Marilyn

Marilyn

RICHARD HAVERS & RICHARD EVANS

**CHARTWELL
BOOKS**

Brimming with creative inspiration, how-to projects, and useful information to enrich your everyday life, Quarto Knows is a favorite destination for those pursuing their interests and passions. Visit our site and dig deeper with our books into your area of interest: Quarto Creates, Quarto Cooks, Quarto Homes, Quarto Lives, Quarto Drives, Quarto Explores, Quarto Gifts, or Quarto Kids.

This edition published in 2017 by
CHARTWELL BOOKS
an imprint of The Quarto Group
142 West 36th Street, 4th Floor
New York, NY 10018 USA
www.QuartoKnows.com

© 2017 by Greene Media Ltd.

ISBN-13: 978-0-7858-3535-6

Printed and bound in China

10 9 8 7 6 5 4 3 2 1

Design: Greene Media Ltd

Compiled, written, and designed by
Richard Havers and Richard Evans.

Any Internet site information provided was correct when provided by the Authors. The Publisher can accept no responsibility for this information becoming incorrect.

PHOTOGRAPHY

Every effort has been made to trace the copyright holders. We apologize for any unintentional omissions, and would be pleased, if any such case should arise, to add an appropriate acknowledgement in future editions.

Front Cover: 506265822 © Shaw Family Archives/Getty Images; Back Cover: 42-17134687 © Sunset Boulevard/Getty Images; 14: 42-17134690 © Sunset Boulevard/Sygma/Corbis; 17: 42-19420547 © Lebrecht Music & Arts/Corbis; 9: 42-22778604 © Sunset Boulevard/Corbis; 6: 0000317473-002 © Sunset Boulevard/Corbis; 2: U1314996INP © Bettmann/Corbis; 41: 42-16079288 © Julien's Auctions/epa/Corbis; 43: 42-17458483 © William Carroll/Corbis; 23 : IH158479 © Corbis; 35: U244758ACME © Bettmann/Corbis; 38: U631684ACME © Bettmann/Corbis; 44: 42-16655700 © Michael Ochs Archives/Corbis; 21: U696209INP © Bettmann/Corbis; 68: 42-20208861 © Aquarius Collection/Sunset Boulevard/Corbis; 47: 9000054880-004 © Sunset Boulevard/Sygma/Corbis: 95: 42-19151812 © Cat's Collection/Corbis; 75: 42-20563038 © Sunset Boulevard/Corbis; 50: VV865 © Underwood & Underwood/Corbis; 78: PEN3848 © Underwood & Underwood/Corbis; 92: U935272ACME © Bettmann/Corbis; 85: U1161065INP © Bettmann /Corbis; 88: U1191870INP © Bettmann/Corbis; 102: U1204146INP © Bettmann/Corbis; 98: U1480578 © Bettmann/Corbis; 134: 42-15979863 © Michael Ochs Archives/Corbis; 124: 42-17134684 © Sunset Boulevard/Sygma/Corbis; 137: 42-18806263 © Cat's Collection/Corbis; 117: 42-19654086 © Sunset Boulevard/Corbis; 127: BE054277 © Bettmann/Corbis; 110: JA005341 © James L. Amos/Corbis; 120: JS9837 © John Springer Collection/Corbis; 104: U1050732 © Bettmann/Corbis; 138: U1119675 © Bettmann/Corbis; 108: U1314975INP © Bettmann/Corbis; 146: 42-17134685 © Sunset Boulevard/Sygma/Corbis; 161: 0000380394-009 © Sunset Boulevard/Corbis; 140: BE032251 © Bettmann/Corbis; 143: BE036936 © Bettmann /Corbis; 162: U1198384 © Bettmann/Corbis; 156: U1350021INP © Bettmann/Corbis; 167: 0000267484-001 © John Bryson/Sygma/Corbis; 181: BE001157 © Bettmann/Corbis; 174: BE032129 © Bettmann/Corbis; 170: SF16254 © Bettmann/Corbis; 176: U1282850 © Bettmann/Corbis; 186: 42-20425226 © Cat's Collection/Corbis; 32: 2694772 © Getty Images; 71: 2716724 © Getty Images; 56: 53372507 © Time & Life Pictures/Getty Images; 67: 73996453 © Michael Ochs Archives /Getty Images; 60: 74283955 © Michael Ochs Archives /Getty Images; 130: 3204884 © Getty Images; 115: 3244301 © Getty Images; 179: 2666795 © Getty Images; 183: 53376357 © Time & Life Pictures/Getty Images; 5: imw0123337 ©2005 TopFoto/ImageWorks; 18: rv15656-14 © Roger-Viollet / Topfoto; 107: © Melinda Mason; 72: © Derek Anthony Collection; 164: © Derek Anthony Collection; All ephemera courtesy of the Dix Archive.

CONTENTS

How Norma Jeane became Marilyn

'First, I'm trying
to prove to myself
that I'm a person.
Then maybe I'll
convince myself that
I'm an actress.'
~ **Marilyn**

PROLOGUE

'If I am a star, the people made me a star.'
~ Marilyn Monroe in her last interview

IN 1998 MARILYN MONROE was voted *Playboy* magazine's Sexiest Female Star of the Twentieth Century. Some may argue with such an accolade, but many millions would agree. It's just one of hundreds of plaudits that have been awarded to Marilyn during the, almost, fifty years since her tragic death. A year after the *Playboy* award, in an auction of Marilyn's personal effects at Christie's in New York at what was called 'The Sale of the Century,' millions of dollars were spent by collectors all eager to own a piece of her. Around the world there are more Marilyn Monroe impersonators than of any other celebrity. Her movies are watched on DVD, TV, and cable channels in just about every country on earth and there are more tribute sites on the web to her than any other actress — alive or dead. There have been numerous books written about her 36 years on earth; all try to make sense of her appeal while trying to make sense of her life.

The enduring fascination of Marilyn can, in part, be put down to the fact that no one has ever quite understood her. She managed to be a little girl lost, while at the same time being outrageously sexy. She was vulnerable, yet she flaunted her body. At times she craved acceptance as an actress, yet in her last, unfinished, movie she took her clothes off — happy to appear naked. Was she a great actress or was she just stumbling through, just being herself? According to Sir Laurence Olivier, one of her co-stars and a great actor himself, "She is a brilliant comedienne, which to me means she also is an extremely skilled actress."

Marilyn lived the majority of her life on the outside. As a child she was unwanted by a mother who spent much of her life in a psychiatric hospital; Marilyn was never sure who her father was. Married three times, she was unable to be what her husbands wanted her to be. They had been attracted by what they saw and then wanted to change her into something she was incapable of being. She never found the kind of happiness with a man that she dreamed of, yet she never behaved in a way that would allow a man to completely trust in her.

Hollywood was also attracted to what they saw, they tried to make her be something that they could manage and manipulate into making them money. Marilyn was never happy with that and at times fought against it, with the result that she was never really accepted by Hollywood. She was a natural talent who constantly tried to be something different. She was also hurt by Hollywood; she blamed them for her problems. Marilyn was no different to the rest of us; it's often easier to blame others.

Marilyn's last interview with a *Life* magazine journalist is heartbreaking. You hear a woman who is at times unsure, at times sad, at times clearly grasping for the strands of reality. What you also hear is nothing like the 'little girl lost voice' that she so often adopted as her public persona. She also revealed that she would love to have been like a normal person – a cleaning woman. Being allowed to do the things that ordinary people do without having to be 'Marilyn Monroe.' Once she said goodbye to Norma Jeane the chances of ever having what passes for a normal life were lost forever. Above all else, Marilyn does not sound entirely sober. Whether it was drink or drugs, who can say, but many years earlier Marilyn had set off down the complete opposite of the mythical yellow brick road. Sometimes people do not decide these things, they just happen

Yet despite her human frailties, her failings, and her problems Marilyn's memory is cherished by millions of people the world over. Ever since her death, at a comparatively young age, there have been countless conspiracy theories; theories that have prevented some from remembering how she was a talented, yet fragile, actress. From 'poor little orphan girl' to a worldwide celebrity, this is the story of how Norma Jeane became Marilyn Monroe and captured the imagination of the world.

'I was never used to being happy.' ~ Marilyn Monroe in her last interview

THE DATES OF HER LIFE

A Marilyn Timeline

The dates given for films are those of their US premieres.

1926

1 June: Born Norma Jeane Mortenson, baptized Norma Jeane Baker in Los Angeles County Hospital.

1935

Norma Jeane is sent to a Los Angeles orphans' home when her mother is placed in an institution.

1942

19 June: Norma Jeane marries James Dougherty.

1944

Norma Jeane starts work at Radio Plane Munitions.

1946

19 July: Norma Jeane has a screen test.

August: Norma Jeane signs contract with 20th Century-Fox and becomes Marilyn Monroe.

September: Marilyn divorces James Dougherty.

1947

4 January: *The Shocking Miss Pilgrim.*

7 December: *Dangerous Years.*

August: Dropped from her 20th Century-Fox contract.

1948

March: Contract with Columbia Pictures.

11 March: *Scudda Hoo! Scudda Hay!*

1 February: *You Were Meant For Me.*

3 June: *Green Grass of Wyoming.*

1949

10 February: *Ladies of the Chorus.*

May: Does nude photo shoot with Tom Kelley.

12 October: *Love Happy.*

1950

18 April: *A Ticket to Tomahawk.*

23 May: *The Asphalt Jungle.*

6 October: *Right Cross.*

7 October: *The Fireball.*

13 October: *All About Eve.*

December: Signs a new contract with 20th Century-Fox.

1951

18 May: *Hometown Story.*

15 June: *As Young As You Feel.*

10 October: *Love Nest.*

31 October: *Let's Make It Legal.*

JOE DI MAGGIO, *Yankees*

1952

March: First date with Joe DiMaggio.

March: The nude calendar story breaks.

April: First *Life* magazine cover.

16 June: *Clash by Night.*

11 July: *We're Not Married!*

18 July: *Don't Bother to Knock.*

7 August: *O. Henry's Full House.*

5 September: *Monkey Business.*

October: Marilyn makes her radio debut.

1953

21 January: *Niagara.*

June: Marilyn's prints are left outside Grauman's Chinese Theater, Hollywood.

1 July: *Gentlemen Prefer Blondes.*

13 September: First live TV appearance on *The Jack Benny Show.*

4 November: *How to Marry a Millionaire.*

December: First edition of *Playboy.*

1954

14 January: Marriage to Joe Di Maggio.

February: Honeymoon in Tokyo.

February: Entertains troops in Korea.

30 April: *River of No Return.*

16 December: *There's No Business Like Show Business.*

September: Shoots the famous skirt-blowing scene for *The Seven Year Itch.*

Late September: Split from DiMaggio.

November: The 'Wrong Door Incident.'

December: Forms Marilyn Monroe Productions.

1955

February: Starts working at the Actors Studio, New York.

8 April: Interviewed by Edward R. Murrow on *Person to Person* TV show.

3 June: *The Seven Year Itch*.

May: Begins dating Arthur Miller.

October: Granted a divorce from Joe DiMaggio.

1956

April: Marilyn performs a scene from *Anna Christie* at the Actors Studio.

May: Marilyn on the cover of *Time* magazine.

29 June: Marries Arthur Miller.

July: Flies to London to film *The Prince and The Showgirl*.

31 August: *Bus Stop*.

1957

13 June: *The Prince and the Showgirl*.

August: Marilyn suffers a miscarriage.

1958

August: Begins filming *Some Like It Hot*.

November: Finishes filming *Some Like It Hot*.

December: Marilyn's second miscarriage.

1959

29 March: *Some Like It Hot*.

September: Marilyn meets Soviet Premier Khrushchev on the set of *Can-Can* at 20th Century-Fox.

1960

February: Marilyn awarded a star on the Hollywood Walk of Fame.

March: Receives a Golden Globe for *Some Like It Hot*.

8 September: *Let's Make Love*.

1961

January: Divorces Arthur Miller.

1 February: *The Misfits*.

February: Marilyn enters psychiatric hospital in New York.

1962

March: Wins a Golden Globe for World Film Favorite.

March: Spends weekend at Bing Crosby's home in Palm Desert. President Kennedy is also there.

April: Starts work on *Something's Got To Give,* which is never completed.

19 May: Sings 'Happy Birthday' for President Kennedy at Madison Square Garden, New York City.

5 August: Marilyn is found dead at her home.

8 August: Marilyn's funeral at Westwood Medical Park Cemetery.

THE HOLLYWOOD BLONDE BOMBSHELL

'Dietrich made sex remote, Garbo made it mysterious, Crawford made it agonizing, but Monroe makes it amusing. Whenever a man thinks of Marilyn, he smiles at his own thoughts.' ~ **Milton Shulman**

IT WAS JEAN HARLOW, Marilyn's idol during her early years, who became known as 'the blonde bombshell.' The phrase came into popular usage as a result of Harlow's film *Bombshell* that had its premiere in 1933. She had earlier appeared in the Frank Capra-directed *Platinum Blonde* so it's easy to see which way the Hollywood moguls were heading with her image.

By the time *Bombshell* was released in Britain the phrase had so captured the public's imagination that it was retitled *Blonde Bombshell*.

'Lovely, luscious, exotic Jean Harlow as the Blonde Bombshell of filmdom.'

Harlow was born Harlen Carpenter in Kansas City, Missouri in 1911; she married at 16 and by the time of her second film, *Red Dust*, her second husband had committed suicide. As a result of her success in films that included Howard Hughes' *Hell's Angels,* the sale of peroxide rocketed in America as women across the country dyed their hair; with home peroxiding many efforts ended in failure which made some women cut their hair really short. Harlow's career lasted for ten years, before she died from uremic poisoning at the age of 26.

Initially the term 'blonde bombshell' was colloquially used in a euphemistic sense to describe a sex symbol; this was back in the days when it was not acceptable to use the word 'sex' other than as a gender-descriptive term. By the time of World War II it was used to denote the nose art painted on the United States Army Air Forces bombers that mounted the daylight raids on Nazi Germany.

Marilyn took the concept of the blonde bombshell to a whole new level when she dyed her hair a much lighter shade, shortly after meeting her agent, Johnny Hyde. Prior to Marilyn, and in addition to Jean Harlow, we think of Greta Garbo, Betty Grable, and Mae West as typical blonde bombshells. Betty Hutton was another one, although in her case it was a comment on her comedic talent rather than her looks or sexiness. Hollywood during the 1930s and 1940s was constantly in pursuit of pretty blonde things to adorn their films, and later on, Britain got in on the act when Diana Dors vied for the title of Britain's blonde bombshell.

Jean Harlow, the original blonde bombshell

Little Girl Lost

1926–1946

On 1 June 1926 a baby that her mother would name Norma Jeane was born in a charity ward of a Los Angeles hospital. It would be the start of a journey through life that would see the girl go from being unwanted by anyone to wanted by everyone.

FAMILY ROOTS

'People respect you because they feel you've survived hard times and endured, and although you've become famous, you haven't become phony.' ~ **Marilyn**

MARILYN MONROE, like just about every actress of her generation, and many others, had a different birth name. The name on her birth certificate is Norma Jeane Mortenson; but like so much of what passes for the facts that surround the life of one of the movies' most legendary actresses it's not remotely true. Ask most people to give Marilyn's real name and they can usually come up with Norma Jeane, thanks to Elton John's ode to Monroe, 'Candle in the Wind.' Some will be able to tell you her surname was, for a while, Baker, which is also true, for Marilyn was baptized Norma Jeane Baker. It's all very confusing. Was the name Monroe a figment of a Hollywood studio's PR department? The truth is far less imaginative.

Marilyn Monroe's maternal family originally hailed from the Midwest, a small rural community in Missouri. Her grandmother Della Mae Hogan's family were less than enthralled when she married a man 13 years older than herself – he was also far from a great catch. Otis Elmer Monroe was a bit of a drifter who had come to Missouri from Indiana in search of work, mostly of the manual kind. At the start of the 20th century the Monroes headed to Mexico where Otis had secured work with the Mexican National Railway, and it was in the border town of Porfirio Diaz ((now known as Piedras Negra) that Marilyn's mother, Gladys Pearl Monroe, was born in May 1902.

By all accounts it was like many border towns, a difficult place to live with none of the kind of comforts even someone from the rural Midwest was used to. Otis soon began to get

itchy feet again and talked to his wife about taking their baby daughter north to Southern California and the attractive-sounding, relatively urban City of Los Angeles.

Norma Jeane Mortenson's birth certificate, dated 1 June 1926

An orange grove in Los Angeles in 1902 which will later become the busy section of Hollywood Boulevard and Western Avenue

THE CITY OF ANGELS

'Los Angeles the City of the Angels – or to give the sonorous Spanish title, Nuestra Senora la Reina de Los Angeles – the Wonder city of the United States, is the most talked-of city on the continent.'

~ Los Angeles Chamber of Commerce brochure, 1915

THE MONROES HEADED NORTH early in the 20th century. Back then, Los Angeles it was a long way from the sprawling city of nearly four million that it is today. There were around 200,000 people living there and it had grown quickly following the discovery of oil in 1892. When the Monroes rented an apartment in the south of the city, oil was already being produced; by the time Marilyn was born it was supplying over a quarter of the world's demand.

Los Angeles had already earned itself something of a negative reputation as the 'city of lost demons.' It was very much the poor relation to the 'Paris of the West,' as San Francisco was known. It was right around the time that the Monroes moved to Los Angeles that they had another child, a boy they named Marion Otis Elmer Monroe. Within a year, San Francisco suffered its earthquake in April 1906 and three-quarters of the city was laid waste and more than half its population of 400,000 were left homeless. Some moved south to what they saw as the safety of Los Angeles and Southern California. Even by 1910 Los Angeles was still being referred to as something of the poor relation. An entry in the 1910 Standard Dictionary of Facts states '... Los Angeles, on the Los Angeles River, 480 miles south of San Francisco.'

Not that Otis ever got the chance to read the Standard Dictionary of Facts. He was dead. Not long after the family moved to Los Angeles Otis fell ill, which his wife thought was more a result of his heavy drinking than any specific medical condition. While the family moved from one rented apartment to another Otis grew worse, complaining of headaches, which were followed by seizures. Since moving back to America, Otis had been employed by the Pacific Electric Railway, the company whose streetcars would provide most of the transportation to and from Hollywood between 1920 and 1940. Sometime around 1908 he was promoted, which enabled the family to buy a home at 2440 Boulder Street in the Boyle Heights area of the city.

Within a year Otis had been admitted to hospital, so bad had his seizures become and so erratic was his behavior. He was diagnosed with syphilis and on 22 July 1909 the grandfather that Marilyn would never know died. Della Monroe was 33 years old and her daughter Gladys had just had her seventh birthday; little Marion was not yet four years old. By all accounts Della stayed in the house and kept body, if not soul, together by entertaining widowers, and in early 1912 she accepted a proposal of marriage from Lyle Graves, who had worked alongside Otis at Pacific Electric Railway. However, far from guaranteeing them a roof over their head, Graves lost his job and couldn't get another, which meant that the family lost its home too. Shortly after this, husband and wife split up for a while. Despite trying to reconcile their differences, and getting back together for a time, which seemed to arise from

Oil rigs in Los Angeles, 1907

Graves making no effort to find work, they split up for good and Della went back to calling herself Monroe.

By the time Gladys was 11-years-old her mother and brother had moved to Venice, an area of the city that sits next to the Pacific Ocean. Della frequented the dance hall on Fraser's new Million Dollar Pier and it was there that Della met Charles Grainger, a widower and oil company worker. Soon they began living together as man and wife to spare their reputations. It was a difficult time for Marilyn's mother who, it appears, was not keen on the idea of her mother and Grainger living together. For whatever reason, little Marion was sent to live with his cousins. For Gladys, her mother's lifestyle, which she completely disagreed with, seemed to act as a spur to seek out a life of her own.

Fourteen-year-old Gladys started hanging out at the pier in Venice where she met 26-year-old Jasper Newton 'Jap' Baker, a man who hailed from Kentucky and worked in his family's merchandise concession on the pier. Ten days before her 15th birthday Gladys Pearl Monroe married the man of her dreams. It was an illegal marriage under California law but Della signed papers saying her daughter was eighteen; Della seems to have worked for Baker, which might have had some bearing on the situation.

America had entered World War I a month earlier and it was a time of uncertainty, yet for Gladys she was certain of one thing. She was going to have a baby. Before the year was out she gave birth to a little boy they named Robert Kermit, although they called him Jack; it was another person added to the population of Los Angeles, which was fast approaching half a million people. It was not the mushrooming birth rate that was driving the growth, it was the influx of people attracted to a city of riches – there was oil, and there were the movies

and the aviation business. The newly-weds lived with Della and Grainger on Coral Canal in Venice. Somewhat confusingly, during this period Della was calling herself Monroe as well as Grainger, getting a passport in 1920 with the latter name, although there is no evidence that she married Charles.

Gladys Baker, as she now was, had a second child in 1919, a girl she named Bernice Inez. Two years later, she was seeking a divorce from Baker as well as claiming she was not really cut out to be a mother. In May 1922, despite a protracted divorce case, the courts agreed that their marriage should end. Sometime earlier in the year, Gladys was back living with her mother at another address in Venice as her mother's relationship with Grainger may have been over, or it may have been because Grainger was away, working abroad. Under the terms of the divorce John Baker had visiting rights, which is why he was able to take the children with him when he left Venice to return to live in Kentucky. What had been a definite case of child abduction turned into an unofficial switch in custody rights after Gladys visited Kentucky and agreed with Baker that he should keep their two children.

Some time after her return, Gladys moved to Hollywood, unable any longer to live with a mother with whom she constantly argued. One reason for Gladys moving to Hollywood was because she had a job in the fledgling film business as a cutter and splicer at Consolidated Film Industries. CFI processed negatives and made prints for motion pictures, and had only been formed in 1924 so it was a very new business. The company, along with numerous others, had grown up around the industry that was fast making Los Angeles the movie capital of America and the world.

Fraser's Million Dollar Pier, Ocean Park, California.

HOLLYWOOD!

'For the ill-advised or headstrong girl who starts for Hollywood with only enough money to buy her ticket, without any particular talent or training, or any assurance of finding work, the best possible thing is being done by the community and the studios. Propaganda is constantly being published warning girls not to embark upon such a foolhardy errand.'
~ **Movie Weekly, March 1922**

HOLLYWOOD IS LOCATED northwest of downtown Los Angeles and about 15 miles from Venice. Films had been made in Los Angeles from around the time the Monroes had moved to California but the first 'Hollywood' studio was located on Sunset Boulevard and was established in 1911. The first film specifically to be made in a Hollywood studio was The Squaw Man in 1914, which was directed by Cecil B. DeMille and Oscar Apfel. By 1915 the majority of films were being made in Hollywood, among them D.W. Griffiths' controversial Birth of a Nation; by 1920 it had become integral to the Southern California economy, employing tens of thousands of people.

The three major studios in Hollywood were Paramount, Warner Bros., and Columbia. Adolph Zukor was the man behind Paramount, who signed early stars including Mary Pickford, Gloria Swanson and Douglas Fairbanks. The Warner brothers, Harry, Albert, Sam, and Jack had, had emigrated from the Polish part of the Russian Empire and established their studio close to Paramount. It was Sam and Jack that produced the pictures while their brothers dealt with the business side of things. It was a dog that put the studio on the road to major success. The company, for a fee of $1,000 per week, signed a dog called Rin Tin Tin, who had been brought to America from France by an American soldier following the end of the war. Harry and Jack Cohn, along with Joe Brandt, founded Columbia in 1919 as Cohn-Brandt-Cohn Film Sales. They released their first feature film in 1922 and in 1924 began calling themselves Columbia Pictures. Gladys would have been well aware of all three companies, along with a myriad of others all desperately seeking to make their fortune.

Silent films were the only movies when Gladys began working in Hollywood. Actors, including comedian Charlie Chaplin who made films for Keystone, Essanay, and Mutual,

were among the highest paid. Buster Keaton, another of the silent screen's major stars, built a $300,000 'Italian villa' home in Beverley Hills, while Clara Bow became one of the movie industry's first female screen goddesses.

Clara Bow and Victor Fleming on location in San Antonio, Texas, where Clara Bow was starring in the 1926 production, *Wings*

HELLO NORMA JEANE

FOR GLADYS, her work at Consolidated Film Industries brought her into contact with Grace McKee, who was single and, like Gladys, was divorced and out for a good time. The two often spent their free time together and before long ended up sharing an apartment not far from their work. Their nightlife was funded by their work, and with her two children off her hands there was nothing holding Gladys back. Soon she met a 27-year-old man named Martin Edward Mortensen, who was a gas fitter for the Los Angeles Gas and Electric Company. Mortensen, a former baker, had been born in Vallejo, California although his father had originally come from Haugesund, Norway. On 11 October 1924, 22-year-old Gladys married Mortensen in Hollywood; theirs would be a marriage that was anything but.

Within no time at all Gladys started a relationship with a lab supervisor at Consolidated, a man named Stanley Clifford who sported a Clark Gable moustache and was by all accounts nearly as handsome. Clifford's wife was divorcing him and it wasn't long before Mortensen was divorcing Gladys. Within six months, Gladys went back to calling herself Baker and to living with Grace McKee. With her divorce through and her freedom regained, Gladys was hopeful that she would soon be Mrs Clifford, or at least living with Stanley as man and wife. The only issue was that he was not so keen on the idea, and as their relationship cooled Gladys had to accept that she was back on the market.

It was at this point that Gladys discovered she was pregnant but was unsure who the father was. Clifford rejected her and so did her mother, to whom she turned for help. Unsure of who the father was, and either scared or unable to bring herself to have an abortion, 24-year-old Gladys gave birth to a baby girl at 9:30am on 1 June 1926 at Los Angeles County Medical Center in Boyle Heights. Mother and daughter were in a charity ward. The Beaux-Arts

The statue of Marilyn Monroe in Haugesund, Norway, the town where Mortensen's family had originated

'No one ever told me I was pretty when I was a little girl. All little girls should be told they're pretty, even if they aren't.' ~ **Marilyn**

building that housed the hospital would later become famous, because it featured in the opening scenes of the soap opera General Hospital. Gladys stated that Norma Jeane was her third child but the only one to still be living.

There has been conjecture ever since as to who Marilyn Monroe's father might be. The fact that it says 'Mortenson' on her birth certificate is inconclusive, of course. Clearly the mis-spelling was a either mistake on the registrar's part, or happened because Gladys told him that was how her husband spelled his name. It could be that Gladys wanted to avoid any stigma of illegitimacy for her daughter; she was still legally married to Mortensen and it would be another year before the divorce came through. Some have speculated that she may still have been having a sexual relationship with Mortensen. Clifford is another possibility – it's been said that he offered Gladys money while she was pregnant; whether this was from guilt or through kindness is unclear.

"Marilyn told us how she had recently gotten a man's name from that orphan asylum. Her mother had listed a Mortensen as her biological father. The night she had finished The Asphalt Jungle, after the wrap party... she called information in some place like Whittier, got the man's phone number and called it... She was convinced that this man was her biological father, and she explained to the man who she was... A drunken male voice responded, 'Listen you tramp, I have my own family, and I don't want anything to do with Hollywood bums. Don't you ever call me again.'" – Shelley Winters

In the 1950s Marilyn wrote an autobiography with Ben Hecht, the American screenwriter, director, producer, playwright, and novelist. In it she talks of being shown a photograph of a man with a small 'Clark Gable-like' moustache that her mother said was her father. Her mother also said that he was killed in a car accident in New York City.

BEN HECHT

Born in 1894, the man known as 'The Shakespeare of Hollywood' always denied he wrote Marilyn's autobiography. His screenplays added up to 70 films and he wrote 35 books. The *Dictionary of Literary Biography* calls him 'one of the most successful screenwriters in the history of motion pictures.' His screenplays included *Scarface* (1932), *Some Like It Hot* (1939, and nothing to do with Marilyn's film of the same name) and *Casino Royale*. The autobiography, cunningly entitled *My Story*, was ghost written by Hecht sometime in 1954 and was clearly designed to capitalize on Marilyn's success through publishing the story as a series of magazine articles. According to Hecht's reports to his editor, he was sure that Marilyn fabricated parts of the story. He was sure that it was not a deliberate lie, but the result of her fantasies.

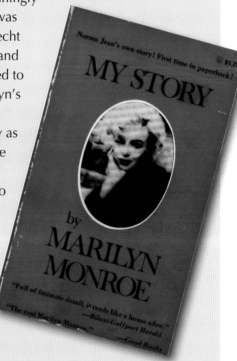

'My childhood was an extension of other people's expectations. I never had any control over what was going to happen to me.' ~ **Marilyn**

Marilyn's description of his relationship with her mother is a somewhat rose-tinted love story.

In some ways Marilyn's fantasies about her father were totally explicable. A father whom she did not know would, as it would for anyone, prove difficult for her to deal with, but at the same time she had to cope with the knowledge that her mother did not want her. Gladys' mother seems to have been pivotal in the situation that developed and ended with baby Norma Jeane being given away. Grandmother Della had neighbors in Hawthorne who would be perfect people to bring up the baby; they were apparently good Christian people. Gladys paid Ida and Albert Bolander $25 a month to look after Norma Jeane. Bolander was a postman and he and his wife were regular churchgoers with a disinclination toward drink and cigarettes. But, and it's a long shot, perhaps both grandmother and mother recognized their instabilities? Then again, do any of us know that we're mad?

With her baby safely in the hands of the Bolanders, Gladys lived once more with Grace McKee – the two of them by now working at RKO; Gladys was a film cutter. Some biographies have stated that young Marilyn had vague remembrances of her grandmother. While Della probably did visit the Bolanders, it seems impossible for Marilyn to have any recollection of her grandmother because she died when

Marilyn was 14 months old. Della is said to have died in a straightjacket at Norwalk State Hospital, but others deny that is the case. Whatever the truth, according to Ida Bolander she was prone to unusual behavior that some would consider 'mad.' Gladys made the funeral arrangements for her mother and had her buried next to Otis Monroe, her first husband.

Gladys would visit Norma Jeane at the Bolanders and, according to Marilyn in later life, she referred to her as 'the woman with the red hair.' By most accounts, Gladys was beginning to have issues with her state of mind that would plague her life. Marilyn remembered being concerned about her, even frightened by her, when she sometimes visited Gladys' apartment and spent time with Grace McKee and her daughter. Confusingly, Gladys is listed at living with the Bolanders in the 1930 census, which is shortly after Ida Bolander told Norma Jeane to stop calling her 'mom' and her husband 'dad.' Marilyn later recalled that Ida Bolander said her mother was the lady with the red hair.

Marilyn's life with the Bolanders came to an end following a bizarre incident. She had been allowed to keep a stray black-and-white dog, which she said followed her to Washington School and would wait outside all day until she had finished. One day, in front of Norma Jeane, a neighbor killed the dog with a hoe. It was shortly after this that Gladys took her away

Gladys Pearl Monroe, Marilyn's mother

from the Bolanders and had her come to live with her. This was probably in the summer of 1933, when Marilyn was eight years old and her mother had managed to save enough as a down payment on a three-bedroom bungalow close to the Hollywood Bowl; whether it was the incident with the dog or timing that precipitated Marilyn's removal from the child-minding Bolanders is unclear.

It seems that for a while Gladys and Norma Jeane shared what passed for a normal life. They would visit Hollywood Boulevard and do what most mothers and daughters do. Everything was fine until Grace lost her job; the difficulties of the Great Depression affected every industry, even Hollywood. To cope with the financial demands of her Hollywood bungalow, Gladys took in a couple of English bit-part actors named Atkinson, one of whom was a stand in for George Arliss, the Academy-Award-winning English actor, as lodgers. There is also talk that they acted as child-minders for young Marilyn. While her mother had worked peripherally in the movie business, the Atkinsons were a direct link with the movies and it was them who first showed Norma Jeane a movie magazine, one of many that were so popular with audiences eager to learn every last detail of what seemed like the fairy-tale lifestyles of movie stars.

There was talk of another small-time actor who also came to lodge with Gladys, Norma Jeane, and the Atkinsons. His name has been lost to history but it seems he may have molested Norma Jeane. What is also confusing is the fact that by this time the house may no longer have belonged to Gladys and had somehow come into the ownership of the Atkinsons, and it was they who leased the room to the other actor.

It was sometime after this that Gladys was taken to Metropolitan State Hospital in Norwalk, a southeastern suburb of Los Angeles. She was there in January 1935 and was diagnosed with paranoid schizophrenia. For a while Norma Jeane lived with the Atkinsons, but at some time she moved in with Grace McKee, probably following a spell in a state orphanage after the Atkinsons left Hollywood. Gladys was moved to Agnews State Hospital in Santa Clara County where she was to stay until after the end of World War II. Norma Jeane was never to live with her mother again; she was not yet nine years old.

Top: Toddler Norma Jeane; Center: Lester Bolander and Norma Jeane, known as 'the twins'; Bottom: Norma Jeane

A Chicago soup kitchen during the Great Depression

A LOW DISHONEST DECADE

'A LOW DISHONEST DECADE', is how the Anglo-American poet W.H. Auden described the 1930s, and the difficulties facing virtually every family in America from soon after Norma Jeane was born were a result of the Depression. To have lived through the Depression in America was a life-changing experience for those old enough to comprehend what was happening; Norma Jeane was too young to understand it, but she felt some of its effects and it could have been a contributory factor in her mother's declining health.

The Depression touched, and in some cases devastated, every stratum of society, but as always it was the poor at the bottom of the heap that had nowhere to go – neither up nor farther down – that suffered most. Even today, the very words 'Wall Street Crash' create a feeling of unease and impending doom; media commentators use them as shorthand. The first crash was on 24 October 1929, when Norma Jeane was three years old. The Depression that followed impacted every aspect of life – from business through to entertainment.

The U.S. economy had gone into recession some six months before the October crash, yet no one forecast its severity or even dared to imagine the consequences. In fact, the Depression lasted for much of the 1930s, becoming the longest and most severe so far experienced by the Western world.

The fall in the value of American stocks and shares was catastrophic; by 1932 they were worth 20 per cent of their 1929 value. While it was individuals who suffered most, banks and other financial institutions were for a long while in free fall. By 1933 nearly half of America's 25,000 banks had collapsed, and at the same time almost 30 per cent of the working population were jobless. Collapse on such a grand scale produced a nationwide loss of confidence, which led to drastically reduced spending. It was more a case of 'panic not-buying' with spending on nonessentials cut to a minimum, and even essential purchases becoming luxuries. As a consequence, production fell too; by 1932, output had fallen by 54 per cent. This all led to industrial, commercial, and personal misery on a scale that has never been repeated in the developed world.

Such was the decline in the Southern California economy that in 1929 the Los Angeles Chamber of Commerce stopped encouraging workers to migrate to the city. They instead issued dire warnings: "While the attractions for tourists are unlimited, please advise anyone seeking employment not to come to Southern California, as natural attractions have already drawn so many capable, experienced people that the present demand is more than satisfied."

The 1932 Olympic Games were held in Los Angeles; the city was the only bidder for the honor, but many countries could not afford to send teams and for the host city it was a long way from the money-spinning venture it is today. They did reportedly make a $1 million profit, but this was a contemporary figure that was used to 'talk up' their effect.

President Herbert Hoover, the only head of state never to

"If I went to work in a factory the first thing I'd do would be TO JOIN A UNION"

Franklin D Roosevelt

CIO DEPT. OF EDUCATION AND RESEARCH

have attended the opening ceremony of an Olympics to be held in their country, publicly underestimated the impact of the Depression. In 1930 he told Americans to remain confident: "The fundamental business of this country, that is, production and distribution, is on a sound and prosperous basis".

In the 1932 presidential election Hoover's opponent was Franklin D. Roosevelt. He offered the people a choice, although he was short on specifics, but he did have one key advantage – he was not Herbert Hoover. What Roosevelt offered was termed the 'New Deal'; while he may not have ended the Depression, he was credited by many with saving their jobs, their homes and even their lives. No president since has so dominated the political landscape. Re-elected three times, Roosevelt died in office in April 1945, aged 63.

'This great nation will endure as it has endured, will revive and will prosper. So first of all, let me assert my firm belief that the only thing that we have to fear is fear itself – nameless, unreasoning, unjustified terror which paralyzes needed efforts to convert retreat into advance.'
~ **Franklin D. Roosevelt's inaugural address, Washington, DC, Sunday 4 March 1933**

President Roosevelt, Miss Margaret Lehand, Presidential Secretary, and Mrs. Roosevelt, December 1933

REJECTED TEENAGER

'At twelve I looked like a girl of seventeen.' ~ **Marilyn**

LIVING WITH GRACE McKEE was a much happier existence for Norma Jeane. Grace, as well as working in the movie business, loved the glamour and the romance of the cinema and filled her friend's daughter's head with stories of the film greats. She would take Norma Jeane down to Grauman's Chinese Theater where she encouraged her to put her hands in the hand imprints in the concrete, in particular Jean Harlow's. Norma Jeane collected pictures cut from movie magazines, and while it's easy to link that with who and what she became, so did hundreds of thousands of girls across America and around the world.

Grace had married a man named Ervin 'Doc' Goddard, ten years her junior, who listed his occupation as 'actor' in the 1936 census when they were living in Van Nuys in the San Fernando Valley, a short distance over the hills from Hollywood. It was yet more association for both Grace and her young charge with the world of cinema that they both loved. One of Goddard's three children had come to live with them so Norma Jeane had a playmate. However, it was a situation that was not to last for either of them. By 1938, Grace was briefly separated from Goddard and it's likely that it was around this time that Norma Jeane was placed in the Los Angeles Children's Home Society, an orphanage. Grace would sometimes visit her, on one occasion bringing her a copy of Life magazine with Jean Harlow on the cover, and according to Marilyn in her autobiography she was also sent to foster homes for periods of time. She was 12 years old.

There have been claims of Goddard molesting Norma Jeane, which may also have had something to do with Grace and Goddard separating, although that was only temporary. Another family that Norma Jeane stayed with were relatives, the children of her mother's brother, Marion. Apparently, some years earlier Marion had disappeared. Later still, she moved in with an aunt of Grace into what was another very unsatisfactory situation born from necessity. Some accounts speak of Norma Jeane being disliked while others say she did find a boyfriend, a boy named Bob.

It was in 1938 that Norma Jeane Baker, as she was now calling herself, first had contact with her half-sister Bernice, who was living in Kentucky and was married. Norma Jeane was around 12 years old and she began writing letters to Bernice in her neat handwriting. She talked of movies and music and fashion like most girls her age, she always finished her letters with the words 'your sister'. There were even attempts by Grace and Goddard, who were back together for at least some time in

'She always wanted to go to the movies or talk about the movies.' ~ **Marilyn's boyfriend Bob**

'I'm going to be a great movie star some day.' ~ **Marilyn**

1939, to get Norma Jeane to Kentucky to meet her sister and possibly to have her live with them. It was totally unworkable as Bernice lived in a two-room apartment.

Sometime in late 1941, Goddard got a job in West Virginia and Grace went with him; they could not take Norma Jeane because she was still a ward of court because of her mother's incarceration in a mental institution. Not that Gladys was too insane to sit back and do nothing about it. She was well enough to write to Bernice in Kentucky asking her to help get her removed from Agnews State Hospital. Neither would Norma Jeane have been happy to go with Goddard, and with no prospects of living with Bernice, who was by now a mother of a young baby, Norma Jeane seemed to be in desperate straights.

Grace hatched a plan with her neighbor Ethel Dougherty. It involved some matchmaking of the most unusual kind. The Doughertys had a son, a 20-year-old lad named Jim who worked in the aviation industry. Apparently, with Grace's encouragement he had taken 15-year-old Norma Jeane to a dance at Christmas 1941, three weeks after Japan attacked Pearl Harbor and America entered World War II.

Hollywood Boulevard at Vine Street, December 1941

GOODBYE NORMA JEANE

'All those guys chasing after her, taking pictures of her.
I wanted her to be a wife... I wanted a normal life. She didn't.'
~ Jim Dougherty

SHORTLY BEFORE WAR BROKE OUT Los Angeles was a city of over one-and-a-half million people. Grace and her husband moving East was very much against the grain. Most people were coming to Los Angeles, where there had been a massive surge in the job opportunities as American industry was in full swing, supporting the war effort of Britain and her allies who were fighting Nazi Germany. Against this background of a booming local economy prospects for a 20-year-old like Jim Dougherty had never been better; at work there was unlimited overtime and away from the daily grind he would have appealed to many young women in search of a husband.

Norma Jean and Jim Dougherty's wedding day

Jim married Norma Jeane on 19 June 1942 at the home of an attorney friend of Grace and her husband; she had just had her sixteenth birthday. Jim knew some of his wife-to-be's unusual background before they married. No doubt while encouraging the relationship Grace let certain information slip, and it's said she told Norma Jeane to tell her future husband all about her mother and her grandmother. No matter how it was told, a young man from what appears to have been a relatively stable background like Dougherty's would have been shocked at some of what he heard. Norma Jeane's itinerant lifestyle, the madness in her family, and the unusual situation surrounding her siblings would have created an image that, had she not been so pretty, would have put many a young man off marrying her.

For the newlyweds the one thing that seems not to have been a great success was their sex life. Marilyn was a virgin, but the incidents in her childhood had left their scars. With an older, perhaps more sensitive man, things might have been easier but it could not have been straightforward for a young man like Jim to be patient with a wife as physically attractive as Norma Jeane. However, against this background they do seem to have been happy together initially, and by February 1944 they were living on Catalina Island where Jim was undergoing training following his call-up into the merchant marine.

Photographer or Studio ___W. O. Schwartz___

Address ___426 So. Spring St___

For value received, I hereby consent that the pictures taken of me by the above named photographer on ___5/18/45___ at ___426 So. Spring___ or any reproduction of them, may be used or sold by said photographer for the purpose of illustration, advertising or publication in any manner without limitation or reservation. I hereby certify and covenant that I am twenty-one years of age or over.

Signed ___Norma Jean___
Model

___Lee Bush___

One of the first photo shoots with Marilyn, taken on 18 May 1945 by W. O. Schwartz. She was not yet 21-years of age

'An American dream girl.'
~ photographer Bob Shannon,
who took pictures of Marilyn in 1946

After Jim went to sea, Marilyn moved back to Los Angeles to live with his parents. While Jim was away she learned to drive and, most importantly, got a job. Like many American women, Norma Jeane worked to support the war effort. She found work at the Radio Plane Company; they made radio-controlled pilotless aircraft that were used for target practice. Initially she was packing parachutes, but soon her part in the process was to spray the varnish onto the lightweight fabric used to construct the aircraft. It was unpleasant work with the smell of varnish and glue constantly in the air.

Women working on the home front often attracted photographers keen to portray how the war had changed things so much for them, especially if they worked in unfamiliar roles. If a women was pretty so much the better, which is exactly what the Army photographer who arrived at the Radio Plane Company thought when he saw Norma Jeane. His name was David Conover, and before the war he had had a studio on Sunset Boulevard. Soon he was getting Norma Jeane to pose away from the factory environment, and before long Jim Dougherty was getting very upset.

Mrs Norma Jeane Dougherty in *Yank* magazine, 26 June 1946

Conover showed the pictures to another photographer, and it was following this that Norma Jeane was introduced to Emmeline Snivley, the owner of the Blue Book Modeling Agency. That was the moment when everything changed.

By early 1945, with Jim Dougherty still at sea, Norma Jeane had left her in-laws house; she stayed briefly with a relative before living at the Hollywood Studio Club. In the meantime, she had lightened her hair considerably on the advice of another photographer she worked for. It was on 26 June 1946 that Norma Jeane appeared on the cover of Yank magazine, photographed by David Conover; by the end of the year, she and Dougherty were divorced. Twenty-year-old Norma Jeane was on her way, even if at that point she wasn't sure where exactly she was heading.

A Blue Book modelling shot of a brunette Norma Jeane taken by David Conover in Castle Rock State Park, California, July 1945

Daring to Dream

1946–1950

Like many other stars, Marilyn trod the tried and tested path from model to the movies. However, for every one that makes it hundreds are left behind, and as Marilyn's story unfolds it's clear that her success is a mix of luck, a little bit of who-you-know, some of who-you-kiss, and possibly a touch of who-you-go-to-bed-with. A conventional route to the top or otherwise, Marilyn is no overnight sensation.

COVER GIRL

'Norma Jeane was a refreshing natural.'
~ William Carroll, photographer, 1945

NORMA JEANE BAKER'S success as a model had come at the cost of her marriage to Jim Dougherty; yet it seems likely that, even given the fact that in the mid-1940s divorce was not so commonplace, it would not have lasted. His jealousy, along with her family history and her age when they first married, mitigated against a long and happy marriage.

The now-single Norma Jeane shared a room with another aspirant at the Hollywood Studio Club, and according to that girl she was posing in some of the more risqué magazines, which in itself was risky for Norma Jeane's ambitions. It could have prevented her from getting straight modeling work, but such was the camera's love for her that she found herself working constantly. It's been said that what attracted Norma Jeane, more than anything else, to the whole business of modeling was the acceptance that it brought her. From being an unwanted teenager she had become a 20-year-old in great demand. There were bathing suit sessions, underwear sessions, and cheap magazine covers; there was anything and everything that needed a beautiful girl to attract buyers. While the magazines may have made money, and the photographers did all right by all accounts, the models did not; it was far from lucrative work and quantity was the byword, not quality.

Other girls who lived at the Hollywood Studio Club report that Norma Jeane was quiet, and while not exactly keeping herself to herself she was not one to join in with the others. Some talk of her being withdrawn, strange even; certainly she was nothing like the woman she became. There was talk of her not sleeping well, even taking tablets to help knock herself out.

Some, especially other models who were not getting as much work as Norma Jeane, speculated that she must be sleeping with one or some of the photographers or those who decided who was to be photographed. One even asked her flat out if she was sleeping around in order to get work. Norma Jeane was indignant. "Of course I'm not," she told the other model. "What kind of girl do you think I am?"

It was not just in America that Marilyn was featured in magazines. She worked with photographer Andre de Dienes, who took a series of shots of her during a month-long trip to Washington State at Christmas 1945 and sold the images worldwide. Additionally, and extremely plausibly, it has been claimed that Norma Jeane and de Dienes were lovers, which puts her indignation into context. On 13 April 1946, she appeared as a flower picker on the cover of a British magazine called *Leader*. This was before her first-ever cover shot on America's *Family Circle* magazine.

Norma Jeane Baker in 1947

FOXY LADY

'In Hollywood a girl's virtue is much less important than her hair-do.' ~ **Marilyn**

IN *MY STORY* Marilyn talked of her life when working as a model. "The Hollywood I knew was the Hollywood of failure. Nearly everybody I met suffered from malnutrition or suicide impulses." This is at odds with what others who knew Norma Jeane, and worked as models, said life was like in that post-war period. She talked of eating at drugstore counters, and certainly it was a life anything but the glamorous idyll portrayed in magazines by those aspiring to be more than just models, those attempting to break into the big time. To her, Hollywood was a place of lies, half-truths, and deceit. But life was certainly no worse than it had been when Norma Jeane the unwanted teenager – the 'child-bride' as she called herself in later years – was a varnish-sprayer in an aircraft factory.

modus operandi was to use the back entrance to the MGM studios as a short-cut to the casting couch in an office that strangely didn't even bear his name.

Within a month of making the cover of *Yank* magazine with the photograph taken by David Conover, Norma Jeane had her first serious opportunity to make the move from modeling to movies. When precisely she decided that this was what she wanted to do is unclear; her own version of her life in those pre-fame years is as much fiction as fact.

In order to get a divorce from Jim Dougherty, Norma Jeane spent six weeks in Las Vegas to secure the necessary residential qualifications to complete it quickly. It was on her return that she had a meeting with Ben Lyon, on 17 July 1946

Among the men she met was a Hungarian named Lazlo who offered to arrange her marriage to a millionaire, a millionaire who, Lazlo reckoned, would die within six months after the wedding and Norma Jeane would inherit everything. "That's like murder," said Norma Jeane. But according to her, he was one of the less sleazy opportunists, especially when compared with one of Sam Goldwyn's talent scouts. His

at 20th Century-Fox; the 45-year-old Lyon had been an actor and was now an executive at the studio. She was naturally nervous and, according to Lyon, answered his questions with a 'forthright honesty.' While that was in her favor, the fact that she had done no acting was not. The story goes that Lyon asked to see her because of the 'couple of dozen' magazine covers that she was on. This seems unlikely, given the fact that

'Jean Harlow all over again.' ~ **Ben Lyon**

BEN LYON

Born in Atlanta, Georgia, Ben Lyon, like many actors of his generation, went to Hollywood and the movies from the New York stage. He came to prominence in the silent film Flaming Youth. He worked with some of the silent

screen's leading ladies including Gloria Swanson and Mary Astor before having his most successful role opposite Jean Harlow in *Hell's Angels*, a story of World War I fighter pilots. It's been said that his playing opposite Jean Harlow is what impressed Marilyn the most when she met him. In 1930 he had married actress Bebe Daniels and they were a well-known Hollywood couple, acting together in films and in Britain on the BBC's long-running radio series *Hi Gang* and later in *Life with the Lyons*. Ben Lyon died in 1979, eight years after Bebe Daniels.

Ben Lyon was impressed with what he saw. He liked the fact that she seemed unconsciously to combine innocence and an allure, bordering on out-and-out sex. He immediately arranged to show her screen test to Darryl F. Zanuck, the man who had founded Twentieth Century Pictures in 1933 before buying out Fox Studios to become 20th Century-Fox. He was, by all accounts, a man who had a prodigious appetite for beautiful young starlets and so on paper Marilyn should have been just perfect. Instead, 44-year-old Zanuck was less than impressed. He considered her just another pretty model who was not really worth wasting their time on. Lyon was convinced otherwise and he persisted, and eventually Zanuck relented, agreeing to let his Head of New Talent have his way.

'Zanuck is the only man who can eat an apple through a tennis racquet.' ~ David Niven

Norma Jeane initially signed a minimum contract with Lyon, who paid her $75 per week, which is more reasonable than the $125 that many biographers claim. That would equate to close to $120,000 a year today, which seems too much. She had, in the recent past, earned anything from £20 to $50 a day for her modeling assignments, but that, of course was freelance – feast or famine work. Whatever the terms of the deal, Norma Jeane had her foot on the first rung of the movie ladder. She signed her contract at the end of August, two weeks before her divorce to Jim Dougherty was finalized.

she had not featured very often on covers at that point. More likely is that either the Hollywood grapevine (which most of the photographers she worked with were wired into) or someone else tipped off Lyon about her.

Impressed by Norma Jeane's openness, Lyon decided to do a screen test with her. Two days later, she was back at 20th Century-Fox where they took some silent color footage of her walking, sitting, and moving in and out of shot. The cameraman that day was Leon Shamroy, who would later film her in *There's No Business Like Showbusiness*.

'She had a kind of fantastic beauty, like Gloria Swanson.' ~ Leon Shamroy

Filming on the lot at 20th Century-Fox studios

M.M.

FOR THE PURPOSES of her contract with 20th Century-Fox, Norma Jeane was no longer Norma Jeane Baker, although on the day she signed it she was still technically Mrs Norma Jeane Dougherty. In *My Story* Marilyn perpetuates the myth that she was still calling herself Mrs Dougherty, but all the evidence points to this not being the case. In the same book she tells an elaborate story about her aunt telling her, for the first time, that her grandmother's name was Monroe and how she was related to the fifth president of the USA, James Monroe. According to Norma Jeane's aunt Grace, Gladys was, 'directly descended' from the early-19th-century president.

The precise truth about how Norma Jeane became Marilyn Monroe we'll probably never know. Alliteration certainly can work really well, and as we all now feel so comfortable with the notion of Marilyn Monroe it sounds just perfect. It's likely that Ben Lyon had a hand in it, probably with a little help from his protégé. However, it was no instant decision; for a little while Lyon called her Carole Lind, but this did not last. Almost immediately after signing for Fox, Marilyn got her first part, although it was a very small one that would go unnoticed because she went uncredited when the movie was released in early 1947.

The Shocking Miss Pilgrim (1947)

A musical based on the life of a late-19th-century stenographer named Miss Pilgrim, who wins over her good-looking boss as the first female employee at a Boston shipping office. Although the men object to her at first, she soon charms them all, especially the handsome young head of the company. Their romance gets sidetracked when she becomes involved in the women's suffrage movement. All ends happily ever after when Miss Pilgrim and Mr Pritchard reunite and later marry.

The music was composed by George and Ira Gershwin, and according to Frederica Sagor, who wrote the screenplay and later became one of the infamous 'Hollywood 10,' "Not even if they had scraped the very bottom of the barrel could they have come up with something so unmelodious."

'Miss Grable and Mr Haymes are neither given nor deserve a script if the caliber of their performances is a valid criterion, and several other minor actors behave ridiculously in silly roles.' ~ *New York Times*

It may just be possible that Marilyn said, "Hello," in the film; she was cast as a telephone operator.

CAST & CREDITS
Betty Grable – Cynthia Pilgrim
Dick Haymes – John Pritchard
Anne Revere – Alice Pritchard

Director – George Seaton
Producer – William Perlberg
Witten by – George Seaton
Music – Alfred Newman
Cinematography – Leon Shamroy
Studio – 20th Century-Fox

SEARS

FREE PARKING

FOR SEARS CUSTOMERS

The Fox Village Theater in the LA suburb of Westwood, 1948

SHE SPEAKS

'A movie job hunter in Hollywood without a car is like a fireman without a fire engine.' ~ **Marilyn Monroe in My Story, but undoubtedly from Ben Hecht's pen.**

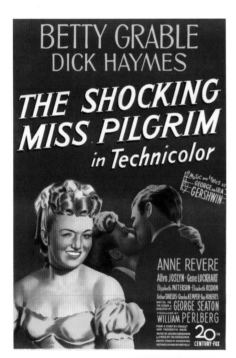

AT ABOUT THE TIME *The Shocking Miss Pilgrim* came out, Marilyn had her first column inches in a newspaper. They talked of her being signed to 20th Century-Fox after she had baby-sat for a studio executive! It also talked of her going to 20th Century-Fox's acting school before being assigned a role. She had obviously been in front of the camera, so to give them the benefit of the doubt they may well have been referring to her first speaking part; then again, it was more a question of typical movie fluff stuff. It was all part of the process orchestrated by Ben Lyon and his department of creating an image, building a profile and to some extent seeing if there was a bite from the press. It's a game that Hollywood played to perfection and Marilyn was a willing participant.

In *My Story* Marilyn speaks about the Hollywood parties she went to during her early years; unquestionably she would have been invited and happy to attend. Many contract actresses were on contract for just such a reason. On one occasion she talks about going to a party with another bit-part actor in order simply to eat because they had had no money. It's more fiction to camouflage the facts.

The work Marilyn did for her weekly wage was hardly onerous. Most reports talk of Marilyn being given a six-month contract. This was extended because she did a number of films for 20th Century-Fox that were released before the middle of 1948. Given that she signed her first deal at the end of August 1946, it seems likely that it was extended for at least another six months and possibly longer; Marilyn herself later talked of her 'year' at the studio.

Read virtually any biography of Marilyn Monroe and it will tell you that her first speaking role was in a film called *Scudda Hoo! Scudda Hay!* Even Marilyn says so in *My Story* and in other retrospective interviews about her career. "I didn't have an opportunity to do anything actually during the year that I was there at 20th Century-Fox the first time, except one part at *Scudda Hoo! Scudda Hay!*, and then they dropped me."

Now it just possible that Marilyn made *Scudda Hoo! Scudda Hay!* before she made *Dangerous Years,* but the latter film was released before the movie that many claim was the one in which she made her speaking debut; some even claim it to be her on-screen debut, which was very evidently *The Shocking Miss Pilgrim. Dangerous Years* provided Marilyn with just a single day's work, although as a contact actor she got paid whether she was on set or not.

Throughout this period Marilyn also took acting lessons, paid for by 20th Century-Fox, at the Actors' Lab behind Schwab's drugstore on Sunset Boulevard; she was there around the same time as Audie Murphy who was working hard to shed his Texas accent. From all available reports it appears she did not show huge promise during these lessons.

Dangerous Years (1947)

Not only was Marilyn Monroe's on-screen presence barely felt, it lasted all of 22 seconds, but neither was the film itself. Running out at just 62 minutes it's a simple, moral, film in which a character named Jeff Carter starts a boys club that helped put an end to some bad behavior in a small town. Everything is fine until a young man named Danny Jones arrives and uses his force of personality to influence Willy, Doris and Leo. They hang out at a café/bar where Marilyn's character, Evie, works as a waitress. Danny goes to trial after he shoots Jeff Carter who tries to stop a robbery the young thug has planned. The trial conducted by the District Attorney is vigorous but the defense say the ones that are at fault are the young man's parents. After the boy is given a life sentence it turns out that he is the DA's long lost son.

'Some of the causes of juvenile delinquency, and some of the adult policies designed to offset them, are explored interestingly here in a melodrama forcefully directed by Arthur Pierson.'
~ *Motion Picture Herald*

Marilyn's role as waitress Evie called for her to walk through the crowded café to the bar and say,
"Six more all-day sundaes."
At which point a young guy comes up to her.
"Hi, Evie."
"Hi, Small change." Says Marilyn
"I got money tonight; am I gonna see you later?"
"If I'm not too tired."
"But Evie I thought we had a date?"
"Look, this tray weighs a ton," says Marilyn as she pushes past the young man.

CAST & CREDITS
Billy Halop (as William Halop) – Danny Jones
Scotty Beckett – Willy Miller
Richard Gaines – Edgar Burns
Ann E. Todd – Doris Martin
Donald Curtis – Jeff Carter

Director – Arthur Pierson
Producer – Sol M. Wurtzel
Witten by – Lamar Trotti
Screenplay – Arnold Belgard
Music – Rudy Schrager
Cinematography – Benjamin Kline
Studio – 20th Century-Fox

One of a series of promotional stills of Marilyn, 1948

SHE SPEAKS... AGAIN

A MONTH BEFORE *Scudda Hoo! Scudda Hay!* premiered in March 1948, Marilyn is reported to have appeared as an uncredited 'flapper' in *You Were Meant For Me*. This musical, directed by Lloyd Bacon and starring Dan Dailey and Jeanne Crain, had music by Alfred and Lionel Newman. She was effectively just an 'extra'; given that Marilyn was, by the time this film was made earning somewhere closer to $100 a week, 20th Century-Fox were just looking to get some return on their investment.

Just why *Scudda Hoo! Scudda Hay!* is claimed to be Marilyn's first speaking role is unclear. It might just have been the first time she was actually filmed speaking in a movie, but there's no question that *Dangerous Years* came out first. It certainly was not Marilyn's first film role as too many biographers suggest. In fact, it was almost a non-event as most of what was shot featuring Marilyn ended up on the proverbial 'cutting room floor.'

Marilyn filmed some sequences in a canoe with Diana Herbert, the daughter of F. Hugh Herbert who also wrote and directed the film. Diana was, like Marilyn, under contract to 20th Century-Fox. According to Diana Herbert, Marilyn was not well regarded at Fox, although according to her father "Marilyn photographed like a million dollars." The scene in which Marilyn appears has her coming out of church while June Haver, the film's star, and Natalie Wood, still a child, are having a conversation; all Marilyn says is "Hi, Rad," and if you blink you will likely miss her.

Marilyn's last film, at least in terms of its release, while under contract to 20th Century-Fox is another attempt to make "agriculture pay," as Bosley Crowther from the *New York Times* succinctly summed it all up. Called *Green Grass of Wyoming* it starred Peggy Cummins, Charles Coburn, and Robert Arthur along with a cameo from folk singer Burl Ives. Once again Marilyn's involvement is uncredited and she appears as a square-dancer in this tale of humans and animals on a ranch, directed by Louis King and adapted from a novel by Mary O'Hara.

'Pleasantly tinted by a battery of 20th Century-Fox Technicolor cameras, it's the sort of picture which doesn't go anywhere in particular, but succeeds well enough in holding attention and leaves one in a genial mood.'
~ **New York Times on Green Grass of Wyoming**

When *Green Grass of Wyoming* opened at the Roxy in New York City in June 1948, the show that went along with it featured headliner Harry Richman, singer, pianist, comedian, and the man who had the original hit with 'Putting on the Ritz'; The Craddocks; Ming and Ling; H. Leopold Spitalny's Choral Ensemble; The Gae Foster Roxyettes and Escorts; Chandra Kaly and his dancers; and the Roxy Theater Orchestra with Paul Ash conducting. All through the 1940s many of the large New York cinemas featured a stage show that played in between the showings of the movie, in this case an 89-minute

feature film. These shows had become extremely popular during the war when there were six or seven shows a day and eleven on Saturdays. The shows started in the morning, some even before 9am. The early shows came about as a result of war work and a combination of factors; people had more money to spend, with less and less to spend it on. The movies and entertainment were prime candidates for their disposable dollars. The need for increased production meant that many factories were working a full 24-hour pattern, many more people, often women given the need for men to join the military, worked shifts, and not just regular shifts, but swing shifts. They worked a week or a month on early shift, then the same on the late shift and finished up the swing through the shifts with a night shift.

Scudda Hoo! Scudda Hay! (1948)

In Britain this color film was known as *Summer Lightning*, no doubt because *Scudda Hoo! Scudda Hay!* meant absolutely nothing outside of America; it actually meant none too much there either and caused some to deride the film. Its title refers to the human call used to rouse mules into action; the film is, among other things, about raising mules and racing them. The farm hand, played by Lon McCallister, who is the man responsible for his boss's mules, is also trying to win his employer's daughter's affections; June Haver is the object of his desire.

'Having long since found the secret of how to make agriculture pay in a series of Technicolored pictures localized on assorted farms, Twentieth Century-Fox is now extending both its formula and its luck in a rather reckless venture entitled *Scudda-Hoo! Scudda Hay!*' ~ *New York Times*

CAST & CREDITS
June Haver – Rad McGill
Lon McCallister – Daniel 'Snug' Dominy
Walter Brennan – Tony Maule
Anne Revere – Judith Dominy
Natalie Wood – Eufraznee 'Bean' McGill

Director – F. Hugh Herbert
Producer – Walter Morosco
Witten by – George Agnew Chamberlain
Screenplay – F. Hugh Herbert
Cinematography – Ernest Palmer
Studio – 20th Century-Fox

Darryl F. Zanuck: "Your type of looks is definitely against you"

SHE SINGS

'You need someone looking after your interests, Marilyn. You're a very attractive and remarkable girl but you can't just run around without someone taking care of you.' ~ **Joe Schenk**

AND THEN MARILYN WAS SACKED. Sacked as a contract actor for 20th Century-Fox in what are confusing and conflicting circumstances. The company had spent somewhere between $4,000 and $6,500 on her during the year she was under contract; that's anything up to $100,000 in today's money. What did they get for that? Three uncredited roles in which the most she said was "hello," and possibly not even that, and two films in which she featured for under 30 seconds of dialogue in total. That would have been fine if it had been all about Marilyn serving an apprenticeship, but at the time few had any confidence in her ability to make it beyond being a pretty face in the background – just a bit-part actor who would not even warrant a footnote in movie history.

According to Marilyn, Darryl F. Zanuck thought she might turn into an actress one day, but "your type of looks is definitely against you." This appears to be the basis on which she was fired from her contract. Not even Marilyn's friendship with Joe Schenk, the 70-year-old who was the absolute head of 20th Century-Fox, could save her. Ben Lyon certainly seems to have been genuinely surprised that it happened. Rumors have persisted ever since as to the real reason. It may have been down to the fact she was having a relationship with another

contract actor who was being lined up to marry one of Zanuck's daughters. Then again, it may have had something to do with Marilyn's reputation as a part-time call girl that she is supposed to have admitted later to being. Whatever the truth, she needed to find some work if she were to continue pursuing her dream of being an actor.

It was during this period that Marilyn did some nude modeling in order to pay the rent. It was a risky business as no studio wanted to work with anyone who had any skeletons in their closet. However, Marilyn had Joe Schenk to thank for helping her to land her next job. He put in that all-important call to Harry Cohn at Columbia Pictures and asked him to give her a six-month contact. Harry obliged and Marilyn was back under contract from March 1948, once again on a minimum weekly wage of $75. She was also back living at the Hollywood Studio Club after a time spent in her own apartment.

After working with one of Columbia Pictures' drama teachers Marilyn got her first break with her new studio. It was a role that not only required her to speak but also to sing. This necessitated some extra lessons that the studio arranged for her to get from Fred Karger, Columbia's Director of

'If my fanny squirms, it's bad. If my fanny doesn't squirm it's a hit. It's as simple as that.'
~ **Harry Cohn on how to rate a movie**

Ladies of the Chorus (1948)

This hour-long film features Marilyn as a showgirl who has a romance with a rich young man that puts her in conflict with her mother, a burlesque dancer. Both mother and daughter dance in the chorus line before Marilyn gets her chance to star in the show, which is when her romance with Rand Brooks' character begins. Promoted as a 'front-row view of the burlesque world' Marilyn gets to sing 'Every Baby Needs a Da Da Daddy' and 'Anyone Can See I Love You,' as well as dueting with Adele Jurgens (dubbed by Virginia Rees) on 'The Ladies of the Chorus.'

Marilyn's songs were written by Lester Lee and Allan Roberts, who might well not be household names but have impressive pedigrees. Among Lee's many successes was the music for the theme to TV's *The Man from Laramie*. Roberts' most well-known song is 'You Always Hurt the One You Love,' made famous by the Mills Brothers.

CAST & CREDITS
Adele Jergens – Mae Martin
Marilyn Monroe – Peggy Martin
Rand Brooks – Randy Carroll
Eddie Garr – Billy Mackay
Nana Bryant – Mrs Adelle Carroll

Director – Phil Karlson
Producer – Harry A. Romm
Witten by – Harry Sauber
Screenplay – Joseph Carole & Harry Sauber
Music – Mischa Bakaleinikoff
Cinematography – Frank Redman
Studio – Columbia Pictures

Music. It was an uphill task because Marilyn was far from a natural. Her biggest problem was not her voice but the fact that she was incredibly nervous about singing in front of people. Karger even took her to friends' homes and had her perform. Soon Marilyn had fallen in love with her music teacher.

According to Marilyn she "… moved from the Studio Club to a place nearer his house so he could stop in on the way to work and home from work. I sat all day waiting for him." It all ended in tears and Karger later married Jane Wyman, the former wife of Ronald Reagan. Ironically, Karger died exactly 17 years to the day after Marilyn.

'One of the brightest spots is Miss Monroe's singing. She is pretty and with her pleasing voice and style, shows promise.'
~ **Motion Picture Herald**

Ladies of the Chorus was released in February 1949, after Marilyn's contract with Columbia had been terminated in the fall. Given that Marilyn's performance was not bad, there are grounds to suggest her being dropped was unfair.

According to Rand Brooks, Marilyn took her mother to the set one day while she was filming. He reported her to be a frail lady, who 'hardly spoke' and was 'nervous.' Marilyn was surprised she was dropped, and so were others including her Columbia drama teacher. Then again her refusal of Harry Cohn's alleged advances of a sexual nature may have had something to do with it.

At about the same time as *Ladies of the Chorus* came out Marilyn got a part in another film, although her appearance was in a minor role. *Love Happy* is a Marx Brothers movie and they had a particular requirement. "Someone I met at a lunch counter told me they were making retakes and needed a girl for a bit part." When she went on set Groucho said to her, "This role calls for a young lady who can walk by me in such a manner as it arouses my elderly libido and causes smoke to come from my ears." Groucho had found the perfect girl.

Not only was Marilyn in the movie but also she was used by United Artists to promote the film. She went to New York, her first trip to Manhattan, where she did some photo assignments as well as going to some of the Big Apple's bigger nightspots. All too quickly New York was over, and she headed to the Midwest to carry on promoting *Love Happy* in altogether less fashionable cities and surroundings before heading home to Los Angeles and an event that would change the course of her career.

Love Happy (1949)

This was just about the last in a long line of Marx Brothers films, and while it began shooting in the summer of 1948 it was not finished until a year later after the production ran out of money for a while. The plot concerns Harpo and Chico helping young Broadway hopefuls while frustrating a diamond robbery. Originally the brothers planned the film to be a solo vehicle to help Chico pay off his gambling debts, but, without all three brothers agreeing to do it, the producers refused to finance the movie. Many regard it as one of the worst Marx Brothers films

'The Marx Brothers are in fine fettle and, as seems to be the case in recent years, they appear to be much better than their material.' ~ *New York Times*

Marilyn's scene lasts just 39 seconds and opens with the line, "Mr Grunion, I want you to help me. Some men are following me." To which Groucho in his inimitable style replies, "I can't understand why."

CAST & CREDITS
Harpo Marx – Harpo
Chico Marx – Faustino
Groucho Marx – Detective Sam Grunion
Ilona Massey – Madame Egelichi
Marilyn Monroe – Grunion's Client

Director – David Miller
Producer – Mary Pickford & David Miller
Witten by – Harpo Marx
Screenplay – Frank Tashlin, Mac Benoff & Harpo Marx
Music – Ann Ronell
Cinematography – William Mellor
Studio – United Artists

Actors and crew, including Harpo and Chico Marx, relaxing with a game of cards between takes of *Love Happy*, 1948

AGENT JOHNNY HYDE

'Not too many in the business had the moxie Johnny had.'
~ George Litto, a William Morris agent with Hyde

NOT LONG AFTER Marilyn came back from her promotional trip in support of *Love Happy,* she went to a party in Palm Springs thrown by Hollywood producer Sam Spiegel where she met Johnny Hyde, an agent with the William Morris Agency. Hyde was of Hungarian descent and was one of those Hollywood behind-the-scenes men who wielded incredible power and influence. Hyde, in his early fifties, was smitten by Marilyn and, despite being ill with a heart problem, he took her on as a client. He had made his name representing Esther Williams, Lana Turner, and also Bob Hope, who he resembled facially.

Hyde housed Marilyn in a hotel, and through his influence he got her a part, albeit a small one, in a 20th Century-Fox Western called *A Ticket to Tomahawk.* While some found it annoying that Marilyn seemed to be eased into a role that had already been cast, others found it totally explicable with Hyde at the helm of her career. Rather than filming in Hollywood some of the movie was shot in Durango, Colorado – dubbed 'the Hollywood of the Rockies.' Some of those appearing in the movie found Marilyn to be the total antithesis of the blonde, sexy starlet that Hyde was trying to fashion. Instead, she came across as nervous and unsure. Hyde, for his part, had got Marilyn to lighten her hair to create her signature peroxide blonde look, and, most importantly, to keep it that way. He also encouraged her to have some minor plastic surgery on her chin to deal with some blemishes, although not her nose, as has been claimed.

A Ticket to Tomahawk (1950)

This color comedy/Western starring Rory Calhoun was not quite a 'blink-and-you'll-miss-her' movie, but Marilyn's contribution was minimal. The plot concerns a train that some are trying to prevent getting to Tomahawk, which director Richard Sale manages to spin out for 90 minutes.

Marilyn's involvement lasts a good four minutes as she sings and dances with three other showgirls. As one British newspaper said at the time. "Is humour international? I've just seen a Hollywood film that makes me doubt it."

CAST & CREDITS
Dan Dailey – Johnny Behind-the-Deuces
Anne Baxter – Kit Dodge Jr.
Walter Brennan – Terrance Sweeny
Marilyn Monroe – Clara

Director – Richard Sale
Producer – Robert Basler
Witten by – Mary Loos & Richard Sale
Music – Cyril J Mockridge
Cinematography – Harry Jackson
Studio – 20th Century-Fox

Marilyn in Johnny Hyde's backyard at 708 W. Palm Drive, Beverly Hills on 17 May 1950

Louis Calhern and Marilyn in *The Asphalt Jungle*, 1950

THE HOLLYWOOD JUNGLE

'She hardly had to open her mouth and I knew she was right for the part. She was exceptional.' ~ **John Huston**

AROUND THE END OF 1949 and the early part of 1950, Marilyn was living with John Carroll and his wife Lucille Ryman; she worked for MGM and it was the Carrolls that took Marilyn to Sam Spiegel's party in Palm Springs. They had a soft spot for Marilyn and were keen to help her in whatever ways they could. This connection proved invaluable when Lucille and Hyde engineered a small role for Marilyn in *The Asphalt Jungle*, a movie directed by John Huston. Before her audition with Huston, Marilyn was extremely nervous. Anxious to please Hyde and the Carrolls, she really worked hard to present herself properly. In the event she had no real reason to worry, Huston was bowled over by her talent.

Meanwhile, Johnny Hyde had split up with his wife and bought a beautiful new home where Marilyn spent time, often with Hollywood big-shots like Spiegel and Bill Wilder. Shooting began on *The Asphalt Jungle* as soon as *A Train to Tomahawk* had finished; it was the start of Marilyn's busiest year, so far, in Hollywood. *The Asphalt Jungle* was released in late May and according to the *New York Times*, "Mr. Huston has filmed a straight crime story about as cleverly and graphically as it could be filmed."

Before 1950 was over, Marilyn worked on three more films, all of which came out within a week of one another in October. There was another for MGM in which she had a small, uncredited, part. Called *Right Cross,* it starred June Allyson and Dick Powell and was directed by John Sturgess. Marilyn played Dusky Ledoux in this black-and-white movie; it's a story of boxing with an undercurrent of racism and infidelity in post-World War II America. Marilyn has the briefest of scenes in a bar in which she is offered a dinner date at Dick Powell's house; the scene lasts less than a minute.

After her cameo in *Right Cross* she made two films for 20th Century-Fox. The first, *Fireball,* was a low-budget black-and-white film about a roller derby star in which Marilyn plays Polly, a groupie. The film starred Mickey Rooney and Pat O'Brien and at least this time Marilyn had her name on the opening title sequence, albeit at the bottom of a list of actors who appeared under the 'with' credit. Marilyn was not at all taken by Rooney. Prior to filming she assumed he was, in real life, something like the characters he played on screen, she was disappointed to find that he was unpleasant; she alleged he was sexually suggestive towards her.

Her final part during the year was a small part in *All About Eve* starring Bette Davis, Anne Baxter, and George Sanders.

'I don't want to make trouble. All I want is a drink.'
~ **Marilyn in All About Eve**

The Asphalt Jungle (1950)

From a novel by W.R. Burnett, the film was nominated for four Academy Awards, including one for Huston's direction. The plot concerns a group of men planning and executing a jewel robbery; filmed on location in Los Angeles and Cincinnati, it creates an impression of an urban jungle. Crooked lawyer Alonzo Emmerich bankrolls safecracker Doc Riedenschneider to gather together a gang of criminals for a major heist. Marilyn plays Angela Phinlay, Emmerich's girlfriend, in this classic film noir.

'Make a note of Marilyn Monroe as the crooked lawyer's girl friend. She's got personality plus.'
~ *The Daily Mirror*, October 1950

In 2008 the film was selected by the Library of Congress for preservation as being culturally, historically, and aesthetically significant.

CAST & CREDITS
Sterling Hayden – Dix Handley
Louis Calhern – Alonzo D. Emmerich
Jean Hagen – Doll Conovan
James Whitmore – Gus Ninissi
Sam Jaffe – Doc Riedenschneider
Marilyn Monroe – Angela Phinlay

Director – John Huston
Producer – Arthur Hornblow Jr.
Witten by – Ben Maddow & John Huston
Music – Miklos Rozsa
Cinematography – Harold Rosson
Studio – 20th Century-Fox

PAGE 11. SUNDAY PICTORIAL, October 8, 1950.

THE NEW FILMS

Marilyn Monroe brings a little glamour into the thriller "The Asphalt Jungle."

THE ASPHALT JUNGLE (Empire). A strong gangster film that suffers from too much chatter. Sam Jaffe, Louis Calhern and Sterling Hayden stand out among the assorted cops and robbers, and Jean Hagen and Marilyn Monroe are a couple of shapely young women who could drive any man to crime. RATING: Good.

Marilyn plays Miss Caswell and got the part despite some opposition from Zanuck, who thought her better suited to comedy; at least he now found her suited to something.

Then in December, Johnny Hyde, the one man who had been unequivocally good and caring towards Marilyn, died in Cedars of Lebanon Hospital on Fountain Avenue, Los Angeles. He believed in her and just as importantly she believed in everything he told her. Marilyn was distraught and created a scene at the funeral with her histrionics. Hyde's children and wife wanted her to stay away, but Marilyn realized she had lost something very precious. Marilyn may have tried to commit suicide in the days following his death. As with so much of her life, there are conflicting reports as to how serious was her intent.

It was a tragic end to a year in which Marilyn had seemed to turn something of a Hollywood corner. Yet it could all so easily be taking her down a road to nowhere without her mentor and guide.

Marilyn sorts out her fan mail shortly after the release of *The Asphalt Jungle*, 1950

Starlet

1951–1952

At the beginning of 1951, Marilyn, then 24 years old, was poised on the cusp of making it. Johnny Hyde had left her with a contract at 20th Century-Fox, but she wanted to be more than just eye-candy; now she wanted to be taken seriously and get the credits.

THE BLONDE DUMBBELL

'She's the blonde dumbbell.' ~ **Darryl F. Zanuck**

THE LOSS OF JOHNNY HYDE from Marilyn's life was a devastating blow, but it also helped fuel the Hollywood rumor mill. Hyde's health problems with his heart were well known and there were those in the film business who found it both easy and even faintly amusing to blame her for her agent and mentor's death. She had for most of 1950 lived in a hotel, paid for by Hyde, and following his death she was obviously unable to continue living that kind of lifestyle. Her film roles were still far too small to provide anything but limited funds for a life that she had been introduced to. To begin with she stayed with Natasha Lytess, the drama coach who she had worked with at Columbia Pictures while making *Ladies of the Chorus*. While Zanuck continued to be cruel in his comments about Marilyn, Joe Schenk seemed once again to be happy to help her and be there to do what he could.

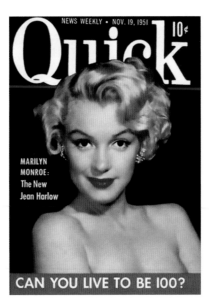

Marilyn had signed a short contract with 20th Century-Fox in mid-December, one that had been arranged by Johnny Hyde, but it did not bode well for her that the head of the studio thought her dumb. There are numerous accounts from the time saying Marilyn was anything but dumb. One actress she worked with said she talked to her about obscure German literature, another said she read Proust, while Marilyn herself enrolled at the University of California, Los Angeles to study literature and art appreciation. Maybe she had heard what Zanuck had had to say about her. However, there were others who agreed with Zanuck and the enigma that was Marilyn began to take shape.

With Hyde gone, Marilyn found it difficult to get anyone to help her at the William Morris Agency. Her relationship with Hyde had probably soured many of those who worked alongside her former agent at what was one of Hollywood's premier talent agencies. Marilyn's former agent Harry Lipton suggested she call Hugh French at Famous Artists Agency and he was more than happy to take her on, along with his partners, Jack Gordeen and Charles Feldman. It was their job to ensure that 20th Century-Fox, and probably Zanuck, in particular, honored her contract and found her roles in the studio's movies or loaned her out to other studios. The only problem was that Zanuck's opinion of her was getting in the way of him signing her to a longer deal. While Marilyn was not exactly washed-up in Hollywood terms, she had 'done the rounds' and so far no one saw in her the potential that a minority did.

'I've had fame. I felt it was fickle.' ~ **Marilyn**

Darryl F. Zanuck's 'blonde dumbbell.' Marilyn on the set of *All About Eve*, 1950

TODAY I MET THE MAN
I'M GONNA MARRY

IN MID-DECEMBER 1950, when Marilyn had signed her new short-term 20th Century-Fox contract, she began work on a new movie for the studio. However, it was just before Marilyn started on the film that Johnny Hyde had died, which made it difficult for her to perform at her best. She had recently spent time working on her acting with the nephew of the Russian playwright Anton Chekov. During her private lessons with Michael Chekov she acted scenes from Shakespeare as well as Chekov's *The Cherry Orchard*. If the stories of her enrolling in UCLA and her acting studies are correct, Marilyn needed and wanted to be seen as more than just a glamorous blonde who appeared in a movie to add a little spice and some eye-candy.

The new Fox picture in which Marilyn had a small part was *As Young As You Feel*, which starred Monty Woolley and Thelma Ritter. It was a long way from the type of role that Marilyn wanted to play, but it did bring her into contact with a man who would play a significant role in her life. Elia Kazan, who was working on his film adaptation of Tennessee Williams' *A Street Car Named Desire,* came to the set of *As Young As You Feel* to see Harmon Jones, its director, who had edited Kazan's *Panic on the Streets* a couple of years earlier. Jones had told Kazan about Marilyn, who a fellow actor on the movie described as being a "pain in the ass half the time."

Accompanying Kazan that day was Arthur Miller, a playwright, communist sympathizer, journalist, and friend of the Hollywood director. Miller was a brilliant writer whose *Death of a Salesman* had been directed by Kazan on Broadway two years earlier; the intellectual Miller was smitten with Marilyn from the moment he laid eyes on her. The only problem was that had been married for ten years to his childhood sweetheart. Marilyn was equally attracted to Miller, and they met again less than a week later at a party at the home of Charles Feldman of Famous Artists Agency. All too quickly Miller went back to living in New York with his wife and Marilyn went back to work on her latest minor film role.

'She had about the worst case of stage fright I've ever seen.'
~ Albert Dekker, who played alongside Marilyn
in As Young As You Feel

As Young as You Feel (1951)

John Hodges is approaching 65-years-old and is told by his boss, Louis McKinley, that he must retire from the printing company at which they work. Instead Hodges decides to impersonate the president of the company that owns the print works and pays a visit to his company. Lucille McKinley falls for Hodges, whose nerves cannot be calmed by his secretary, Harriet, while all sorts of other calamities befall them.

'There is so much that is pleasant about this gay, shrewd and unaffected film, tossed off with a wink and chuckle, that you should try not to let it slip by.'
~ *The New York Times*

Sixteen-year-old Russ Tamblyn also appeared, as one of the McKinley's children. He later starred in *West Side Story* as Riff, the leader of the Jets.

'Marilyn Monroe is superb as his secretary.'
~ *The New York Times*

CAST & CREDITS
Monty Woolley – John R. Hodges
Thelma Ritter – Della Hodges
David Wayne – Joe Elliott
Jean Peters – Alice Hodges
Constance Barrett – Lucille McKinley
Albert Dekker – Louis McKinley
Marilyn Monroe – Harriet

Director – Harmon Jones
Producer – Lamar Trotti
Witten by – Paddy Chavesfsky

Screenplay – Lamar Trotti
Music – Cyril J Mockridge
Cinematography – Joseph MacDonald
Studio – 20th Century-Fox

Marilyn with co-star Albert Dekker in a scene from *As Young As You Feel,* 1951

BREATHLESS IN HOLLYWOOD

'Young Marilyn Monroe, who has logged less than fifty-minutes screen time, stole the show.' ~ **Collier's magazine**

ONE DAY IN EARLY 1951, Marilyn drove herself to Famous Artists Agency office in Hollywood in her Pontiac convertible to meet with Hugh French. He told her he was having little or no luck in extending her contract with 20th Century-Fox. He did however have some good news in that she had been invited to the Fox's Exhibitors' party. It was an event when they brought in movie-theater owners from all across America to meet and greet their finest talent.

Marilyn arrived late for the party a few days later and made what can only be described as – an entrance. "Amid a slowly gathering hush, she stood there, a blonde apparition in a strapless cocktail gown, a little breathless as if she were Cinderella, just stepped from the pumpkin coach." It goes unrecorded what Susan Hayward, June Haver, Tyrone Power, Gregory Peck, and the real Fox stars had to say, but Marilyn was immediately escorted to the table of the President of 20th Century-Fox. Zanuck realized he had been finessed.

It was around this same time that Marilyn was asked to be one of the presenters at the Academy Awards at the RKO Pantages Theater on Hollywood and Vine. Marilyn couldn't have escaped Zanuck's notice; he was there to collect the Irving G. Thalberg Memorial Award, an honor bestowed on 'creative producers.' Zanuck also couldn't help noticing the increase in fan mail for Marilyn that had begun arriving at Fox following the roll out of *All About Eve* across not just America but the world. By May, and partly as a result of all this activity, French had landed a seven-year contract for Marilyn with 20th Century-Fox.

Despite all the ups and downs of the contract negotiations, and perhaps as a result of Zanuck's less-than-enthusiastic opinion of Fox's young contract starlet, Marilyn was loaned to MGM to a make a film. It was another movie that seemed to need a beautiful blonde to fill up some celluloid and so Marilyn got the job. MGM would have paid 20th Century-Fox for the privilege and Marilyn would have got her $500 a week her contract stipulated. But *Home Town Story* was little more than a fleeting few days' work for Marilyn. It premiered on 18 May 1951 and for Marilyn it was a disappointing follow-up to *All About Eve*, which had her much better positioned.

Home Town Story (1951)

It's a story of politics, newspapers, and big business in which left-leaning Blake Washburn, who is seeking re-election to the State Legislature, is defeated. He blames John MacFarland's company and it motivates the former Senator to take over a family-run newspaper so he can pitch it against what he sees as corrupt big businesses. Following an accident on a school trip, Washburn sees for himself the good side of big business. Marilyn plays Iris Martin, a secretary on *The Herald* in this black-and-white film that runs for just over an hour. Marilyn wore a sweater dress that definitely added to her appeal, although she was seen but fleetingly.

The film had some funding from General Motors and was very much at odds with the more liberal-leaning movies that were more often coming out of Hollywood at this time. It is the kind of film that would have languished in obscurity had it not been for Marilyn's appearance

CAST & CREDITS
Jeffrey Lynn – Blake Washburn
Donald Crisp – John MacFarland
Marjorie Reynolds – Janice Hunt
Alan Hale Jr – Slim Haskins
Marilyn Monroe – Iris Martin

Director – Arthur Pierson
Producer – Arthur Pierson
Witten by – Arthur Pierson
Music – Louis Forbes
Cinematography – Lucien Andriot
Studio – MGM

National Screen Services' promotional material for *Love Nest*

MINOR ROLE PLAY

BETWEEN THE RELEASE of *Home Town Story* and *As Young As You Feel* Marilyn celebrated her 25th birthday. With her newly signed seven-year contract and perhaps just a little more realization that the fan mail arriving for Marilyn at 20th Century-Fox must mean something, the studio had her back under their wing for the rest of 1951. There was also talk from, more than about, Elia Kazan putting Marilyn in one of his pictures. Kazan was working on *A Street Car Named Desire*, but it did not stop him spending time with Marilyn, going to parties together and mixing with the Hollywood elite.

Marilyn's next picture was to be *Love Nest*; it's another film starring one of Fox's regular stars, June Haver, with whom Marilyn had worked before. It was to be another minor role, although bigger than she had been used to. According to Marilyn, "In a movie you act in little bits and pieces. You say two lines and they 'cut.' They relight; set up the camera in another place – and you act two more lines. You walk five feet and they say 'cut.' The minute you get a good characterization, they cut." It succinctly sums up the stop-start progress of Marilyn's career in Hollywood and *Love Nest* was to

Love Nest (1951)

"Love Youth? Love excitement? Love rollicking fun? Then most certainly you'll love… *Love Nest*." So said the trailer. It's the story of a writer and his wife, Jim and Connie, who are having problems with their New York apartment building. Bobbie moves in with them, much to the vexation of Connie although Jim's friend Ed is happy. This black-and-white comedy was typical Fox fare and is another film that would now be long forgotten but for Marilyn's appearance.

'A rather dated theme… Marilyn Monroe is tossed in to cause jealousy between the landlords.' ~ *Variety*

The 30-year-old writer of this film, I.A.L. Diamond, was born Itek Domnici in Rumania in 1920. He chose the initials after a magazine editor wanted to put an anglicized version of his name (Ian) next to an article Diamond had written. Settling on I.A.L., which

some say actually stood for Interscholastic Algebra League, his friends called him Iz, but never Izzy. Diamond would later write *Some Like It Hot* with his friend Billy Wilder.

CAST & CREDITS
June Haver – Connie Scott
William Lundigan – Jim Scott
Frank Fay – Charley Patterson
Marilyn Monroe – Bobbie Stevens
Jack Paar – Ed Forbes

Director – Joseph M. Newman
Producer – Jules Buck
Witten by – I.A.L Diamond
Music – Cyril J Mockridge
Cinematography – Lloyd Ahern
Studio – 20th Century-Fox

Let's Make it Legal (1951)

Marilyn's second film under the directorship of Richard Sale was this black-and-white 77-minute comedy drama about the Halsworth's divorce. Victor Macfarland is an old flame of Miriam's and when the Halsworths' daughter and her husband get involved it all becomes a little complicated. Marilyn's billing alongside Barbara Bates belies the fact that her role was a minor one as a kind of Hugh Halsworth groupie. In the trailer Marilyn is referred to as 'Miss Cheesecake herself.'

'I. A. L. Diamond, has aimed some sparkling, sensible dialogue at the American hearth. And Miss Colbert, her colleagues and Mr. Sale have turned it into a real Martini.' ~ *The New York Times,* with no mention of Marilyn

The film also featured Robert Wagner in one of his earliest movie appearances. Fox's 'rousing romance'

also featured Colbert filmed almost entirely from the left side, as was stipulated in her contract.

CAST & CREDITS
Claudette Colbert – Miriam Halsworth
Macdonald Carey – Hugh Halsworth
Zachery Scott – Victor Macfarland
Barbara Bates – Barbara Denham
Robert Wagner _ Jerry Denham
Marilyn Monroe – Joyce Mannering

Director – Richard Sale
Producer – Robert Bassler
Witten by – I.A.L Diamond
Music – Cyril J Mockridge
Cinematography – Lucien Ballard
Studio – 20th Century-Fox

be no different. If not quite a fully fledged star, at least for this film Marilyn featured in the movie theater trailer which shows that 20th Century-Fox were at last alive to her cinematic pulling power. Filming began in April, a month after Marilyn's appearance at the Academy Awards

Love Nest began showing in movie theaters in the middle of October 1951 and was followed two weeks later by the Los Angeles premier of *Let's Make it Legal*, Marilyn's fourth movie of 1951. The timing was perfect as it followed one of the first full-length articles about Marilyn to appear in a national magazine. Prior to this it had mostly been mentions in *Variety*, the trade magazine, film reviews, and the Hollywood gossip columns, although she did make the cover of a smaller magazine called *True Experiences*.

"Do I look happy? I should – For I was a child nobody wanted. A lonely girl with a dream who awakened to find the dream come true. I am Marilyn Monroe, read my Cinderella story." – *True Experiences*, May 1950.

Collier's magazine called their story in September 'Hollywood's 1951 Model Blonde.' The magazine came out weekly and although its readership had dropped from the close to three million it enjoyed right after the end of World War II it still packed a punch, although television was starting to eat into its advertising revenue. A couple of years later *Collier's* was one of the magazines interested in the Ben Hecht-ghosted Marilyn Monroe life story articles that eventually became *My Story*. Marilyn also made *True Romance* in September 1951 so there were definite signs that her star was in the ascendency.

True Experiences
The Magazine About Real People

May

Do I look happy?

I should —
For I was a child
nobody wanted.
A lonely girl with a
dream–who awakened to find
hat dream come true —

84

I am Marilyn Monroe...
read my Cinderella story

Reminiscent of a Vargas girl, Marilyn strikes a cowgirl pose for Valentine's Day, 1951

HOLLYWOOD'S MOST PROMISING

'A forceful actress, a gifted new star.'
~ New York World Telegram

PHOTOPLAY MAGAZINE VOTED Marilyn Hollywood's most promising star in 1952, and it was a vote based on what could best be described as minor roles. However, just five days after the new year had begun Marilyn's world was in danger of crashing down around her. Word of Marilyn posing nude for a calendar photo shoot two years earlier was beginning to leak out and 20th Century-Fox were concerned about how best to play it. Either they could drop their promising star or they could use it to their advantage.

Fox had already loaned Marilyn to RKO Pictures to make Fritz Lang's Clash By Night, which is another indication of their somewhat less-than-enthusiastic support of their starlet. She began work on the film as her rush of 1951 releases were beginning to get general release across America. With all the furore over the calendar there was even talk of canceling Clash By Night, which seems unlikely, as RKO could easily have substituted another actress. Fortunately nothing of the kind happened and Marilyn benefited from what Life magazine described as her "best role since The Asphalt Jungle." Fox did the obvious and chose to stick with Marilyn and when the story of her modeling finally broke in early March for a while the world went nuts for nude Marilyn pictures. Far from damaging her reputation it just upped her collateral to the point where it wouldn't be long before she went from being at the bottom of the list of credited actors on movie posters to the top of the list. As the old saying goes, there's no such

'That gorgeous example of bathing beauty art (in denim) Marilyn Monroe, is a real acting threat to the season's blondes'
~ New York Post

Clash By Night (1952)

Marilyn's part in this film, according to *Variety* was "tantamount to a bit role." It's based on a play by Odets that ran on Broadway in 1941 with Tallulah Bankhead in the star role. Mae returns to the fishing village where she was raised and after staying with her brother Joe, whose girlfriend is Marilyn, Mae marries Jerry, her bother's boss. Jerry's friend Earl is a brutal man but in the second half of the film, which is effectively a two-parter as the action is split by a year, Mae has an affair with Earl, having become bored with her 'good husband' Jerry.

'Clifford Odets' *Clash by Night*, presented on Broadway over a decade earlier, reaches the screen in a rather aimless drama of lust and passion.'
~ Variety

'The Master of Darkness', as Fritz Lang had been dubbed was 60-years-old when he worked with Marilyn. He fled Germany and made his home in Hollywood in 1935 but he was never able to top his masterpiece from the silent film era made in 1927, Metropolis, nor his first talkie from 1931.

CAST & CREDITS
Barbara Stanwyck – Mae Doyle D'Amato
Paul Douglas – Jerry D'Amato
Robert Ryan – Earl Pfeiffer
Keith Andes – Joe Doyle
Marilyn Monroe – Peggy

Director – Fritz Lang
Producer – Jerry Wald & Norman Krasna
Witten by – Clifford Odets
Screenplay – Alfred Hayes
Music – Roy Webb
Cinematography – Nicholas Musuraca
Studio – RKO Pictures

SUNDAY PICTORIAL, July 27, 1952 PAGE 13

'Mr Joe DiMaggio was unexpected.' ~ **Marilyn**

thing as bad publicity just as long as they spell your name right.

In the wake of her loan out to RKO Marilyn was back at 20th Century-Fox for the first of four pictures she would make with the studio before 1952 was over. Marilyn's 1952 releases all came out in what can only be described as a rush. All five movies had their premieres within a less than three-month period, starting with *Clash By Night* on 16 June and culminating with *Monkey Business* on 5 September. *We're Not Married* is about as different a film, when compared to

Clash By Night, as is possible to imagine.

Marilyn, who had just celebrated her 26th birthday, had also met her future husband a few weeks earlier at a dinner date at the Villa Nova restaurant on Sunset Strip. It was a date she almost didn't keep because she had been told he was a baseball star and she felt she would have little to say to such a man. She felt he would probably be brash, boring and possibly worse; in the event, when Marilyn was introduced to Joe DiMaggio she was surprised.

We're Not Married (1952)

A black-and-white movie about five couples who have been married by a newly qualified Justice of the Peace who finds his papers are not in order, so invalidating their marriages, produces five stories within the story. Marilyn's character won the Mrs Mississippi pageant but on learning she is single decides to enter the Miss Mississippi contest rather than the Mrs America competition. Ironically the Gladwyns married for their careers and hate each other.

'The Monroe-Wayne sequence is pretty lightweight, but shows off the Monroe form to full advantage in a bathing suit, offering certain exploitation for film.'
~ *Variety*

Two of the other wives were making early screen appearances. Zsa Zsa Gabor was already on her third husband by the time she appeared in this, her second

movie. It was Mitzi Gaynor's first role for which she had decent billing; she later starred in the film musical *South Pacific*.

CAST & CREDITS
Ginger Rogers – Ramona Gladwyn
Fred Allen – Steve Gladwyn
Victor Moore – Justice of the Peace Melvin Bush
David Wayne – Jeff Norris
Marilyn Monroe – Annabel Norris

Director – Edmund Goulding
Producer – Nunnally Johnson
Witten by – Gina Kaus & Jay Dratler
Screenplay – Nunnally Johnson
Music – Cyril J. Mockridge
Cinematography – Leo Tover
Studio – 20th Century-Fox

Marilyn and Joe DiMaggio on the set of *Monkey Business*. Cary Grant was also in the shot but was deliberately cropped out

THE YANKEE CLIPPER

'What's that you say, Mrs. Robinson? Joltin' Joe has left and gone away?' ~ 'Mrs Robinson' by Simon & Garfunkel

JOE DIMAGGIO and Frank Sinatra were the two great Italian-American heroes of the 1940s. But despite playing baseball for much of his career for the New York Yankees, and unlike Sinatra, Joe was born in Martinez, California on 25 November 1914. DiMaggio's parents had arrived, like hundreds of thousands of others, from Italy by boat, arriving in Ellis Island before settling in California. Papa DiMaggio was a fisherman and when Joe was a year old the family moved to San Francisco.

Joe DiMaggio first played professional baseball for the San Francisco Seals in 1932, but he almost had to give the game up when, in a freak accident away from the game, he tore the ligaments in his left knee. Fortunately, the New York Yankees gave him a try-out and signed him for $25,000, a quarter of what the Seals had expected to get before his accident.

DiMaggio made his Major League debut for the Yankees in November 1936 and that season helped them win the World Series, for the first of four consecutive years; in all DiMaggio won nine titles in the 13 years he played for the Yankees.

During World War II, DiMaggio had joined the army and served from February 1943 until September 1945 as a PE instructor. It was also during the war that Joe's marriage to actress Dorothy Arnold ended. He had met her on the set of *Manhattan Merry Go-Round,* in which he had a small part. They married in 1939 and over 20,000 people thronged the streets of San Francisco to greet them. Two years later they had a son they named Joseph Paul DiMaggio.

However, it was not long before their marriage was in trouble. Joe liked to be with his ball-playing friends while 25-year-old Dorothy felt ignored and was left at home looking after the baby. It all ended in divorce in 1944, with Joe ordered to make maintenance payments of nearly $8,000 per year (around $200,000 today).

By 1949 DiMaggio became the first baseball player to sign a $100,000 annual contract, but Joe was not the player he had been. Injuries had plagued him and he was in so much pain that even walking had become a problem. Aware that he was not cutting it, he retired in December

1951 after reading a Brooklyn Dodgers scouting report that had been leaked to the press. His pride would not let him continue unless he was on top of his game.

'I was full of aches and pains and it had become a chore for me to play. When baseball is no longer fun, it's no longer a game.' ~ Joe DiMaggio, 1951

In 1939 Papa DiMaggio and his three sons opened a fish restaurant on Fisherman's Wharf, San Francisco

Joe DiMaggio never remarried after his divorce from Marilyn. He was a batting coach for the Yankees in the early 1960s and later went into advertising as a spokesman for a bank and for Mr. Coffee. He lived in Florida and helped establish a children's wing at Memorial Regional Hospital in Hollywood, Florida, named after himself. He died on 8 March 1999 in Florida and was interned in Colma, California. DiMaggio last words were "I'll finally get to see Marilyn."

'Dignity, grace and elegance personified.' ~ Dominic DiMaggio, Joe's brother

JOE DIMAGGIO'S BASEBALL CAREER

- New York Yankees debut - 3 May 1936
- Batting average - .325
- Home runs - 361
- Runs batted in - 1,537
- World Series Champion – 9 times; 1936 -1939, 1941, 1947, 1949-1951
- Most Valuable Player - 1939, 1941, 1947
- He holds the Major League Baseball record of 56 consecutive games with a hit
- New York Yankees last game - 30 September 1951
- Inducted into the Baseball Hall of Fame - 1955

A Joe DiMaggio bubble-gum card from the 1938 Goudey 'Heads-Up' series. DiMaggio is not just the most valuable card in the set, it is also one of the most well known and popular of all Joe DiMaggio cards, and of all 1930s bubble-gum cards. They usually fetch from $2,000-$4,000 in auction.

The Yankees' Joe DiMaggio slams one out of the park.

AMERICAN HERO VS. UN-AMERICAN HERO

WHEN MARILYN FIRST MET Joe DiMaggio she had already completed work on two of the three movies that were still to come out in 1952. Many think that Marilyn's blind date with Joe DiMaggio may well have had something to do with Fox's PR campaign to help nullify the effect of the nude photographs. There was, after all, no better all-American hero for Marilyn to be seen with; if she was good enough for the Yankee Clipper she was good enough for America, except possibly if you were a Giants fan. An agent named David March and his wife accompanied the chain-smoking DiMaggio to dinner that night; according to Marilyn, 'Deadpan Joe' as he was nicknamed reminded her of a businessman or a politician. The two of them did not get much of a chance to talk, because Mickey Rooney came and sat at their table and spent most of the evening recounting DiMaggio's exploits to the man who had done them. Joe got Marilyn's phone number and shortly afterwards the two of them had dinner, alone and together.

Marilyn saw Elia Kazan shortly after her second 'date' with Joe DiMaggio and told him all about it.

Elia Kazan's 1952 film of Steinbeck's *Viva Zapata!*

She and Kazan were occasional lovers, and Kazan was in Hollywood to see various friends and colleagues about the hearings for the House Un-American Activities Committee (HUAC), for which he had been subpoenaed to attend. Kazan was going to name names and he wanted to warn people first that he would divulge them to be 'fellow-travelers,' as alleged communist sympathizers were euphemistically known in the early 1950s. Back home in Connecticut, Kazan met with his friend Arthur Miller and told him the news.

Miller's reaction was to visit Salem, in Massachusetts, where he began researching a play based on the infamous witch trials. It became *The Crucible,* which had its opening in January 1953 in New York City. Whereas Kazan named names, Miller, who was also questioned by the HUAC, never did bend to the pressure of 'McCarthyism' and the 'Red Scare.' Kazan went to Europe to direct a movie before returning to Hollywood to make *On The Waterfront,* for which he won an Oscar. His leaving America ended his on/off relationship with Marilyn and left her to the attentions of Joe DiMaggio.

A WICKED SENSATION

'She wasn't shooting a scene with you, you were like participating in a scene with her; like you were a prop of some kind.' ~ **Richard Widmark**

THE FIRST OF MARILYN'S three films to be released in what remained of 1952 was *Don't Bother To Knock*, which had its premiere a week after *We're Not Married*. Marilyn had worked on her new film prior to all the fuss with the nude calendar. Zanuck's view that Marilyn was ready for a better role was made easier by the fact that her role in *Don't Bother To Knock* required her to play a disturbed blonde woman – a role the

Head of Fox felt was made for her. The film was to be directed by Englishman Roy Ward Baker. Baker was 38-years-old when he went to Hollywood to make this, his first American film; he had worked extensively in England for Gainsborough Pictures. Marilyn's co-star was Richard Widmark, who had starred in Elia Kazan's *Panic in the Streets*, so those who like connections are not disappointed.

Don't Bother To Knock (1952)

This 76-minute black-and-white film, adapted from a novel by Charlotte Armstrong, features Marilyn as 'a wicked sensation' and is her first real starring role. The plot concerns an airline pilot, played by Widmark, who meets Nell Forbes who is babysitting for the Jones family; it becomes increasingly apparent that Miss Forbes is the last person who should be looking after Bunny Jones, their daughter. It ends with Jed Towers reconciling with his girlfriend and Miss Forbes exposed as 'the lonely girl in Room 809' as well as being completely deranged.

'They've thrown Marilyn Monroe into the deep dramatic waters, sink or swim, and while she doesn't really do either, you could say that she floats.'
~ *New York Post*

This was Ann Bancroft's first screen role; 15 years later she appeared in *The Graduate* as Mrs Robinson, the subject of Simon and Garfunkel's song in which they reference Joe DiMaggio.

CAST & CREDITS
Marilyn Monroe – Nell Forbes
Richard Widmark – Jed Towers
Ann Bancroft – Lyn Lesley
Donna Corcoran – Bunny Jones
Lurene Tuttle – Ruth Jones

Director – Roy Ward Baker
Producer – Julian Blaustein
Screenplay – Daniel Taradash
Music – Lionel Newman
Cinematography – Lucien Ballard
Studio – 20th Century-Fox

Richard Widmark and Marilyn in *Don't Bother To Knock*, 1952

A WIGGLE
AND A WALK

'However confused and difficult she is in real life,
for the camera she can do no wrong.'
~ Allan 'Whitey' Snyder, Marilyn's make-up artist

THE EXPERIENCE OF WORKING with Roy Ward Baker on *Don't Bother To Knock* was far from a happy one. Perhaps it was the pressure on Marilyn to perform in her first starring role, then again as it was his first Hollywood movie Baker was under some pressure as well. Roy Ward Baker went on to make some interesting movies, including *The Vampire Lovers* and *Quatermass and the Pit*, but he never gained the recognition that Marilyn achieved.

However, before anything further could take place Marilyn was struck down with appendicitis; what worried her most about the operation was the size of the scar. What was worrying the studio executives at Fox was the fact that

Marilyn was growing ever more popular, not at all hindered by the nude photo shoot, and yet she was not the kind of actress that other actors seemed to enjoy working with, nor was anyone at Fox particularly impressed with her intelligence or her personality. Zanuck grew increasingly frustrated and added to his dumb blonde remarks by calling her a 'sexpot.'

He was insistent that the studio give her no more dramatic roles. All he, and many others, thought she was good for was wiggling and walking. *O. Henry's Full House* was therefore just perfect, in the opinion of many of those in charge at Fox. Released on 7 August 1952, it came just three weeks after Marilyn's starring vehicle, which today seems like strange timing in our modern world where movies come much less thick and fast.

'She's a sexpot who wiggles and walks and breathes sex.'
~ Darryl F. Zanuck

O. Henry's Full House (1952)

This unusual idea for a film was an anthology of five stories written by O. Henry, the pen name of William Porter. His stories were always witty, with good characterization and as often as not had a twist in the ending. The story in which Marilyn appeared was called 'The Cop and the Anthem' and it also featured 52-year-old, English-born Charles Laughton and the Tony-Award-winning David Wayne (25 years later Wayne featured in *Dallas*). Marilyn's appearance in the first of the stories was brief but she still received strong billing. While Fox may have had their doubts they understood her box-office appeal.

'Marilyn Monroe, again as sleek as she was in *The Asphalt Jungle*, is a streetwalker of stunning proportions' ~ *New York Post*

The plot concerns the efforts of Soapy, a New York City down-and-out, attempting to get himself put away for three months in jail to avoid living on the streets during the coming winter.

CAST & CREDITS
Marilyn Monroe – Streetwalker
Charles Laughton – Soapy
David Wayne – Horace

Director – Henry Koster
Producer – André Hakim
Screenplay – Lamar Trotti
Music – Alfred Newman
Cinematography – Lucien Ballard
Studio – 20th Century-Fox

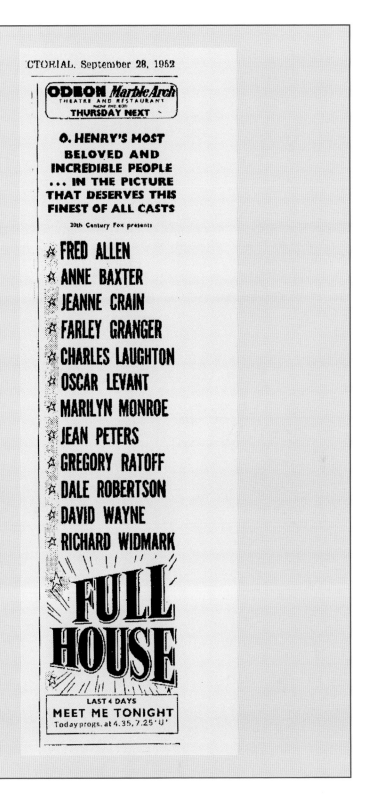

Cary Grant, Ginger Rogers, and Marilyn in *Monkey Business*, 1953

TOO MUCH MONKEY BUSINESS

'Many of the things that seem normal or even desirable to me are very annoying to him.' ~ Marilyn on Joe DiMaggio

MARILYN'S FINAL FILM to be released in 1952 was *Monkey Business*, the movie she was working on when she had her blind date with Joe DiMaggio. By the time the film was in cinemas right across America the newspapers had marriage right across the front pages.

While Marilyn worked on *Monkey Business* DiMaggio visited the studio, which was too good an opportunity for the PR people to miss out on. Cary Grant posed with Marilyn and DiMaggio, but when the photograph was released by 20th Century-Fox they had carefully edited Grant out of the shot, leaving the impression that it was just the two of them.

Besides DiMaggio, who at this point meant nothing to Marilyn, she had been seeing Kazan and there were others. One of these seems to have been quite a serious relationship, conducted both in person and by long-distance telephone calls. He was a young writer who came from Ohio, by the name of Robert Slatzer. They met at 20th Century-Fox and he frequently visited Hollywood where he would meet with Marilyn, behind DiMaggio's back. Over the years Slatzer has talked of his relationship with Marilyn and he even wrote a book about her. His story has not always been taken seriously and many have poured scorn on him. However there are those that have studied his testimony, talked with him and believe that there is no doubt that he was close to Marilyn for most of her adult life.

During the summer of 1952 Slatzer spent a lot of time with Marilyn. He met her on location at Niagara Falls and spent time with her in Los Angeles, which eventually resulted in him being mentioned in a Hollywood gossip column. Much of the tittle-tattle revolved around Slatzer giving Marilyn books to read, books to improve her mind that were the very antithesis of what she was getting from DiMaggio; his love of sports and the boys was not something that was confined to his first marriage. Then, according to Anthony Summers in *Goddess, The Secret Life of Marilyn Monroe*, she and Slatzer were married in a civil ceremony in Tijuana, Mexico. This story is corroborated by witnesses. When Marilyn and Slatzer arrived back in Hollywood, Zanuck, who had been told of the marriage, confronted them and told them it must stop, "For the sake of Marilyn's career and all the money we have invested in her."

Monkey Business (1952)

It was probably while making this film that Marilyn first met Ben Hecht, who would 'ghost' her autobiographical magazine articles that eventually became a book in 1974. He and his close friend Charles Lederer developed what has been dubbed 'the screwball comedy' genre of which this is an early example. It's based around one of life's great quests – the search for the elixir of youth. Fulton is a research chemist who is in charge of the project. He inadvertently takes some of the elixir that one of his chimps, used in his research, has put into the water cooler. Lois Laurel is the secretary to Fulton's boss, a man named Coburn, and she spends the day with Fulton who acts like a 20-year-old rather than a late forty-something.

'Marilyn Monroe can look and act dumber than any of the screen's current blondes.' ~ *New York Daily News*

If the *New York Daily News* were less than impressed with Marilyn's acting ability, *Photoplay* felt very differently: "Typing skill, however, is the only attribute which the lady appears to be lacking in." And while The *New York Herald Tribune* may not have actually called her dumb they did appreciate her assets. "She disproves more than adequately the efficacy of the old stage rule about not turning one's back to the audience. "

CAST & CREDITS
Cary Grant – Dr. Barnaby Fulton
Ginger Rogers – Mrs Edwina Fulton

Marilyn Monroe – Miss Lois Laurel
Charles Coburn – Oliver Oxley

Director – Howard Hawks
Producer – Sol C. Siegel
Screenplay – Ben Hecht, Charles Lederer, and I.A.L. Diamond
Music – Leigh Harline
Cinematography – Milton Krassner
Studio – 20th Century-Fox

Marilyn poses with women from (l to r) the U.S. Army, Navy, Air Force, and Marine Corps, Atlantic City, NJ, September 1952

Home Run

1953–1955

1953 was the year that Marilyn went from being a pin-up, a starlet, and a Hollywood hopeful to fully-fledged film star. *Gentlemen Prefer Blondes* was her first home run, and six months after its premiere in January 1954 she became Mrs Joe DiMaggio and had her first real home.

HAVE YOU SEEN YOUR MOTHER, MARILYN?

'Oh, the calendar's hanging in garages all over town, why deny it? You can get one any place. Besides, I'm not ashamed of it. I've done nothing wrong.' ~ **Marilyn**

'Every wiggle of Marilyn's walk— Get in the queue boys!' —The People

You've never seen anything like— Niagara COLOUR BY TECHNICOLOR

MARILYN MONROE · JOSEPH COTTEN · JEAN PETERS

DIRECTED BY HENRY HATHAWAY PRODUCED BY CHARLES BRACKETT

20 CENTURY-FOX

PLAZA PICCADILLY CIRCUS

PROGS. AT 4.40, 7.25

MARILYN'S FIRST FILM OF 1953 was *Niagara*, which had its premiere in New York City in late January. In the summer of 1952 her role in the film was put under threat, before filming even began, from what some people could be forgiven for thinking was a ghost from the past. Fox's careful management of Marilyn's personal history encouraged most people to think of her as a 'poor little orphan girl.' Gladys, Marilyn's mother, had long since been released from California's state mental institution and by this point was living with relatives in suburban Los Angeles. Gladys' life had continued to be chaotic, not least because she had remarried soon after World War II ended, only to find that her husband was a bigamist with a wife in Idaho.

If all this was not enough, Gladys had become an even more devout Christian than she had been before being sent to the sanatorium; the news of Marilyn's nude modeling was the final straw. For Gladys, even movies were sinful, the devil had manipulated Marilyn into doing his work.

At some point there had clearly been some kind of altercation between Marilyn and her mother, probably encouraging Marilyn to think she was about to break

cover, because she issued a statement to the press through 20th Century-Fox's publicity department revealing that her mother was alive. The statement was somewhat disingenuous in that it hinted strongly at the fact that Marilyn did not know her mother while she was growing up. She also attempted to turn the whole affair to her advantage by announcing, "I haven't known my mother intimately, but since I have become grown and able to help her I have contacted her."

In the wake of the nude calendar 'scandal' Marilyn did not need any potentially harmful publicity, but once again she came out of it all with hardly a blemish on her reputation. There was public sympathy for her and the public liked what they saw on screen, so why doubt what Marilyn had to say about her background? Throughout 1952 men in garages, rest areas, and offices across America were reminded daily of Marilyn because of her nude calendar shots, photographed by Tom Kelley. Rather than a picture a month there was a shot of Marilyn against a red velvet background with monthly tear-off calendars below. Companies paid to have their logos or names on the calendars so they could distribute them to their customers. Tape companies, machinery companies, and crane operators across America all had a hand in promoting Marilyn's career.

Those calendars from 1952 and 1953

Mr and Mrs Frank Conniff, Joe DiMaggio, and Mr and Mrs Toots Shor

UP IN NIAGARA

Marilyn's work on *Niagara* got underway in Hollywood at the end of May 1952. From California she flew to meet up with DiMaggio in New York where the couple spent a lot of time hanging out at one of Frank Sinatra's favorite Big Apple spots – Toots Shor's saloon and restaurant right across from Madison Square Garden. It had been Toots who had taken Sinatra to meet President Roosevelt during World War II; later Sinatra even featured him in a version of 'Me and My Shadow,' with Sammy Davis Jr – Toots was top draw. Toots Shor's was the ultimate New York sports bar and a home-from-home for DiMaggio. Whereas most people shied away from having a woman along with them, DiMaggio was so proud of his new love that he took Marilyn to Shor's, even if Toots didn't really like it. It's unlikely that Marilyn really enjoyed the all-male preserve, but whereas in Hollywood she was not yet a fully-fledged star, in New York with Joe DiMaggio they were a golden couple, even if at this point Marilyn was a rung or two down the celebrity ladder from Joe.

After spending a week or so in Manhattan, Marilyn headed north to Niagara for the location filming of her new movie.

Niagara (1953)

The movie was promoted with the tag line, 'Marilyn Monroe and Niagara, a raging torrent of emotion that even nature can't control.' Henry Hathaway had a reputation for being fierce, but with Marilyn the 52-year-old director came over all fatherly. He was conscious that she was trying really hard to deliver a top-notch performance as the murderer of her husband on a trip to Niagara Falls. Rose and her lover Patrick hatched a plot and the honeymooning Cutlers unwittingly become involved, as Polly is almost killed.

'Here is the greatest star since Jean Harlow. She has more intelligence than Harlow. She out-lures Lana. She makes any other glamour-girl you care to name look house-wifely.' ~ *Los Angeles Examiner*

Marilyn sings 'Kiss,' which she performs in a shocking pink dress. The song was covered by Dean Martin in 1953 and ten years later by Cliff Richard.

CAST & CREDITS
Marilyn Monroe – Rose Loomis
Joseph Cotten – George Loomis
Jean Peters – Polly Cutler
Casey Adams – Ray Cutler
Richard Allan – Patrick

Director – Henry Hathaway
Producer – Charles Brackett
Screenplay – Charles Brackett, Walter Reisch, & Richard Breen
Music – Sol Kaplan
Cinematography – Joseph MacDonald
Studio – 20th Century-Fox

Times Square, New York City, 1952. *Don't Bother To Knock* is playing at the theater next door to Horn & Hardart's Automat

CHEVRO
CRITERION
Walt Disney's
STORY OF
ROBIN HOOD
ALL TECHNICOLOR SHOW!
APITO
THEATR
SUDDEN FEAR
PEPSI

BLONDES HAVE MORE FUN

'Everybody in the studio wanted me as a star in his movie.
I finally went into *Gentlemen Prefer Blondes...*' ~ **Marilyn**

THE STORY GOES THAT Marilyn was told about the film she was to star in after *Niagara* as she celebrated her 26th birthday. If this was the case it would have been as she was preparing to leave Hollywood to fly to New York to spend time with DiMaggio; it would also be before she had begun work on the filming proper. The story of how she got her role in her next film involves Howard Hawks, with whom she had worked on *Monkey Business*. Hawks argued with Zanuck that Marilyn was perfect for light comedy, rather than a psychotic or a murderer that they had cast her as in recent films. Hawks was slated to direct *Gentlemen Prefer Blondes* and as it called for its star to sing and dance, Zanuck was convinced Marilyn was not up to it; Hawks convinced him that Marilyn could do it.

20th Century-Fox had secured the rights to make a film adaptation from what had originally been a Broadway play starring Carol Channing. Besides Marilyn, it needed another strong and glamorous female lead; for Hawks this presented no problem. "Let's use Jane Russell," he suggested to Zanuck. Hawks had directed *The Outlaw*, the film that had launched Russell on to an unsuspecting public. They had remained good friends, while Hawks was also friendly with Howard Hughes, who owned RKO Pictures. The reclusive Hughes often used Hawks' home in Bel Air to conduct his business. Jane Russell was under contract to RKO, so the 31-year-old Miss Russell, who was married to Bob Waterfield, the Los Angeles Rams quarterback, was hired as Marilyn's co-star.

Despite having recently sung 'Kiss' in *Niagara* Marilyn was not really up to sustaining a singing role and so she began taking lessons in order to meet the demands put upon her. Unfortunately, with such a busy schedule of releases as well as filming, Fox seemed to think Marilyn could be everywhere at once and were constantly making her do promotional work. Hawks complained to Zanuck, who agreed that it was stupid for Marilyn to be put under such pressure when they needed her to be at her best to perform alongside Russell in what could be the most important movie of her career.

MARILYN MONROE says

Gentlemen prefer blondes

Hiltone brings glamour to your hair, new exciting glamour that gives dull hair a captivating charm — a charm that makes a man say 'How lovely your hair looks today.'

New fashion ideas with Hiltone . . .

Hiltone gives you just the shade of fairness you need — the very shade — and in the very place you want it too. There's excitement in an alluring blonde streak that ends in a sunkissed curl — magic in suntipped ends that give you a look of sparkling gaiety. Hiltone can give you these new and charming hair fashions in a few minutes, now — this very day.

Hiltone is so easy to use

Hiltone gives you a natural looking loveliness — no-one would guess, even close to, that the secret of your beautiful hair is Hiltone. That's because Hiltone is so gentle — it coaxes the true beauty of your hair to show itself off at its best — it brings out the highlights and sets them dancing. You'll look entrancingly fair with Hiltone.

and blondes prefer

Hiltone
MAKES HAIR FAIR

Hiltone

AT THE NEW LOW PRICE OF 5/7

royds 20/51

Gentlemen STILL prefer BLONDES

Don't be a "mouse" — Brush on

'GOLDEN SHADEINE'

3/1½ at Boots, Timothy Whites, Chemists,

THE SHADEINE CO
Established 60 years
49 Churchfield Road, Acton, Lon

It seems gentlemen prefer blondes in any language

'The bad thing about cheesecake publicity is the letters you get from cranks.' ~ **Marilyn**

Work began on the film that would change everything in November 1952; besides the usual pre-production work, Marilyn was also put through her paces by Jack Cole, a Fox stalwart, who had been tasked with choreographing the movie's dance sequences. While not only having singing lessons but also learning some reasonably difficult dance routines – for an untrained dancer – Marilyn found it all very arduous. New skills, when added to the burden of being the film's star, appear to have brought on a bad attack of nerves for Marilyn. So much so that she would constantly arrive late on set, which frustrated Howard Hawks who considered her unprofessional.

Marilyn got along really well with Jane Russell – even quizzing her on what it was like to have a relationship with a professional sportsman; it seemed to increase the bond between the two stars. Through the course of their conversations Russell realized that Marilyn constantly arriving late on set had nothing to do with poor timekeeping and everything to do with her nerves. Her stage fright also manifested itself in the speed at which she worked, which when combined with her lateness further irritated Hawks. *Gentlemen Prefer Blondes* was beginning to run behind schedule, but on a more positive note Hawks realized that it was well worth it. His hunch that Marilyn was a natural for movie comedy was proving to be right. No one was happier than Marilyn, except possibly Darryl Zanuck.

During the filming of *Gentlemen Prefer Blondes* Marilyn was nominated for an award as 'Best Newcomer' by *Photoplay* magazine. At the ceremony on 9 February 1953 Marilyn wore a sheer gold lamé dress specially made by Billy Travilla, one of Hollywood's leading costume designers. It seemed to accentuate her blonde hair, as well as her figure, and caused quite a sensation. She was also sensational in her acceptance speech, gently purring her lines: "It's a great thrill and I'm very appreciative to everyone who has made this possible." Although it did take her a couple of takes to get it right.

Not everyone approved of Marilyn's dress sense. Joan Crawford told a reporter "It was the most shocking display of bad taste I have ever seen. Look, there's nothing wrong with my tits, but I don't go around throwing them in people's faces. The publicity has gone too far, and apparently Miss Monroe is making the mistake of believing her publicity... She should be told that the public likes provocative feminine personalities; but it also likes to know that underneath it all the actresses are ladies..." In response, Marilyn told legendary Hollywood columnist Louella Parsons that she "cried all night. I've always admired Miss Crawford for being such a wonderful mother – for taking four children and giving them a fine home. Who better than I knows what that means to homeless little ones?"

The filming of *Gentlemen Prefer Blondes* finished a month after Marilyn's appearance at the *Photoplay* Awards and it had been hard work for everyone involved. Marilyn's nerves had been got under control due in part to Jane Russell's encouragement, but mostly it was down to her drama coach, Natasha Lytess. She was on set constantly, arguing with Hawks to allow retake after retake and cajoling Marilyn into improving her performance. Marilyn was also buoyed by the news that *Niagara* had been a major financial success at the box office, grossing four times more than it cost to make.

'Billy Dear, please dress me forever. I love you, Marilyn.'
~ **Marilyn's dedication on a nude calendar to Billy Travilla**

Marilyn at the *Photoplay* Awards in her gold lamé dress designed by Billy Travilla, 9 February 1953

Gentlemen Prefer Blondes
(1953)

The film is an adaptation of a 1949 play that itself was an adaptation of a 1925 novel written by Anita Loos; it had also been a silent movie in 1928. Dorothy and Lorelei, aka Jane and Marilyn, are the lounge-singing 'two little girls from Little Rock', on their way by liner to Le Havre in France. Naturally, on board there are a number of eligible men but Lorelei needs to behave herself in order to win the hand of Gus Esmond, whose father has sent along a private detective, Ernie Malone, to keep an eye on her behavior to ensure that she's good enough to marry his son. Malone ends up marrying Dorothy and naturally Lorelei marries Esmond.

'As usual, Miss Monroe looks as though she would glow in the dark, and her version of the baby-faced blonde whose eyes open for diamonds and close for kisses is always amusing as well as alluring.'
~ *New York Herald Tribune*

While most often remembered as Marilyn's breakthrough movie, Jane Russell gives a stellar performance. Marilyn looks stunning in another shocking-pink dress while performing 'Diamond Are A Girl's Best friend.' In one scene, one of the guys on the ship says to another, "If this ship hit an iceberg those girls couldn't drown."

'There is that about Miss Russell and also about Miss Monroe that keeps you looking at them even when they have little or nothing to do. Call it inherent magnetism. Call it luxurious coquetry. Call it whatever you fancy. It's what makes this a – well, a buoyant show.' ~ *New York Times*

CAST & CREDITS
Jane Russell – Dorothy Shaw
Marilyn Monroe – Lorelei Lee
Charles Coburn – Sir Francis 'Piggy' Beekman
Elliott Reid – Ernie Malone
Tommy Noonan – Gus Esmond
George Winslow – Henry Spofford III

Director – Howard Hawks
Producer – Sol C. Siegel
Screenplay – Charles Lederer
Music – Hoggy Carmichael, Eliot Daniel & Lionel Newman
Cinematography – Harry J. Wild
Studio – 20th Century-Fox

Jane Russell, Charles Coburn, and Marilyn in *Gentlemen Prefer Blondes*

MARILYN'S ROYAL FLUSH

'Celebrities and the man in the street crowd Hollywood's famous boulevard to attend the CinemaScope premiere of *How to Marry a Millionaire,* the first romantic comedy to be filmed in the new miracle medium.' ~ **Movietone Newsreel**

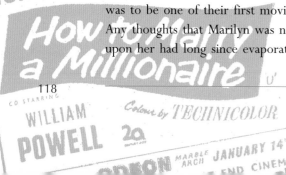

JUST A WEEK BEFORE *Gentlemen Prefer Blondes* had its premiere, Marilyn and Jane Russell left their handprints and their footprints in soft new wet cement outside Grauman's Chinese Theater in Hollywood. They both signed their names and above the 'i' in Marilyn's name there was a rhinestone to commemorate her new film; a thief stole it shortly afterwards and was probably disappointed to find it was not the real thing. It was all part of Fox's carefully co-ordinated promotional campaign to turn their movie into the hit that everyone felt it would and should be. Marilyn was attending the Grauman's Chinese Theater event shortly after completing the shooting of her follow-up film. Her new movie was another in similar territory to her last, although a little more obvious and less subtle. *How To Marry A Millionaire* had commenced filming in March, just four days after she finished filming with Howard Hawks.

20th Century-Fox needed Marilyn in *How To Marry a Millionaire,* despite her tiredness from the demanding schedule she had endured under Hawks. She was big box-office and it was to be one of their first movies filmed in CinemaScope. Any thoughts that Marilyn was not up to the demands placed upon her had long since evaporated after Zanuck and the other

executives at Fox had seen the rough cut of *Gentlemen Prefer Blondes.*

During the demanding work with Hawks Marilyn had begun to take Benzedrine tablets, which not only help suppress the appetite but also give you a mild lift. By the end of the movie Marilyn was noticeably slimmer, a condition aided by the hard work of the dance routines. She also seems to have experimented with taking sleeping tablets during the making of *Gentlemen Prefer Blondes*; Nembutal became her usual drug. In September 1953 Grace McKee, Marilyn's old friend, committed suicide by taking drugs; it may have contributed to Marilyn's increased drug taking.

When *Gentlemen Prefer Blondes* had its premiere on 1 July 1953, Marilyn was at a point where she could renegotiate the terms of her 20th Century-Fox contract. For their part they had already increased her weekly salary to $1,250 (worth close to $1 million per year in today's terms). She was also due to leave for Canada to begin filming her next movie but Darryl Zanuck was also trying to get Marilyn's agreement to filming another movie to follow on immediately afterwards; having found out she could make Fox a great deal of money they were not going to allow Marilyn any respite. Her agent

Charles Feldman was, like Marilyn, not at all keen on the idea of her filming *The Girl in Pink Tights*. He felt that she had reached that point in her career when she at last held the better hand. In the game of Hollywood poker Zanuck may have been the dealer but Marilyn was holding a royal flush.

Back from filming in Canada, Marilyn attended the premiere of *How To Marry A Millionaire* with the film's producer Nunnally Johnson and his wife and Lauren Bacall and her husband Humphrey Bogart, in Hollywood on 4 November. Dressed in a long, strapless Travilla gown she epitomized what we all remember as the 'Monroe look'; soon she would be marrying her very own millionaire.

How To Marry a Millionaire
(1953)

If Howard Hawks helped to make Marilyn a star, then Jean Negulesco, a Romanian by birth who had just made the 1953 version of *Titanic*, helped to keep her there with this typical piece of Hollywood romantic movie fluff adapted from two separate plays by Zoe Akins and Dale Eunson and Katherine Alber. Bespectacled Marilyn, along with Grable and Bacall, play three New York models, Schatze, Pola, and Loco, who share an apartment with the sole purpose of finding and marrying three millionaires. But are the men who purport to be rich really the real deal or are they just impostors? Is love worth more than money? Naturally all three find true love with Wayne, Calhoun, and Mitchell – none of whom are millionaires.

'It is particularly noteworthy that Miss Monroe has developed more than a small amount of comedy polish of the foot-in-mouth type.' ~ *New York Post*

The film was the first to be shown on color TV as part of NBC's *Saturday Night at the Movies* on 23 September 1961.

'The baby-faced mugging of the famously shaped Miss Monroe does compensate in some measure for the truculence of Miss Bacall.' ~ *New York Times*

CAST & CREDITS
Betty Grable – Loco Dempsey
Marilyn Monroe – Pola Debevoise
Lauren Bacall – Schatze Page
David Wayne – Freddie Denmark
Rory Calhoun – Eben
Cameron Mitchell – Tom Brookman

Director – Jean Negulesco
Producer – Nunnally Johnson
Screenplay – Nunnally Johnson
Music – Alfred Newman
Cinematography – Joseph MacDonald
Studio – 20th Century-Fox

Rory Calhoun, Lauren Bacall, Cameron Mitchell, and Marilyn in *How To Marry A Millionaire*, 1953

MRS JOE DIMAGGIO

'I've got to go to Japan on some baseball business and we could make a honeymoon out of our trip.'
~ Joe DiMaggio proposes to Marilyn

SHORTLY BEFORE THE PREMIERE of *How To Marry A Millionaire* Marilyn made her TV debut when she appeared on *The Jack Benny Show*. It was not her very first appearance on the small screen, as she had made a Royal Triton Oil television commercial in 1950. For her performance on Benny's show she wore the Travilla dress she later wore to the premiere of *How To Marry A Millionaire*; she also gently sent up Darryl F. Zanuck, which may have been a subtle form of contract negotiation with Fox. It's a measure of her confidence that she felt able to be so forthright on Zanuck. Before America's eyes Marilyn was becoming Marilyn Monroe, a character of her own making.

Marilyn was finishing up making *River of No Return*, the film she had gone to Banff in Canada to shoot. As if to prove her rising collateral, Marilyn and Charles Feldman had engineered some concessions out of the notoriously difficult Zanuck. As further proof of her star power, when Marilyn clashed with Otto Preminger, the director of *River of No Return,* she was not chastised by Fox, Zanuck, or anyone else. One thing that irritated Preminger was the fact that DiMaggio arrived to stay at the Banff Springs Hotel. It also irritated others working on the movie as they felt Marilyn became distracted. It may have accounted for her unreliability on set when sometimes scenes would take up to thirty retakes. Then to cap it all she hurt her foot while filming a scene in the river, requiring it to be placed in a cast. She was glad to get back to Hollywood, although shortly after arriving home she left to spend time with Joe DiMaggio in San Francisco visiting his old family haunts.

Marilyn was still vacillating, along with her agent, as to whether she should appear alongside Frank Sinatra in *The Girl in Pink Tights*, a remake of a 1943 Betty Grable movie called *Coney Island*. By mid-December Marilyn was supposed to join Sinatra on the Fox lot to begin filming; she failed to show up for

'CinemaScope is very complicated. They have to take out a lot of seats in the cinemas.'
~ Marilyn on the Jack Benny Show, 13 September 1953

work and after a couple of days it became obvious that she was not going to show at all. Meanwhile, Marilyn all but disappeared without trace. She stayed in her apartment for a while with DiMaggio as her doorman; he would let no-one that the studio sent, to try to get her to either change her mind or show up for work, past the front door. Marilyn had finally decided that *The Girl in Pink Tights* was not her kind of movie. Meanwhile, Fox needed her to come to the studio to redo a song for *River of No Return*. Marilyn was frightened to return to the studio for fear it was just a ploy to get her there to try to change her mind about *The Girl in Pink Tights*.

Eventually she did show up to do what was needed, and then immediately left Los Angeles to spend Christmas with DiMaggio in San Francisco. As a present he bought her a beautiful mink coat and by all accounts Marilyn enjoyed what may have been the best Christmas of her life, secure in the DiMaggio family home surrounded by real people who were all relatively normal. Fox, though, had not given up on *The Girl In Pink Tights* and tried to force Marilyn into reporting for work a few days after the New Year. Once again she failed to show up.

Ten days after Marilyn was supposed to be filming with Frank Sinatra at Fox's studio she was dressed in a dark brown coat and walking into San Francisco's City Hall, clutching some white lilies. She was there to marry Joe DiMaggio. Dressed in a blue suit, Joe was already waiting for his bride-to-be, accompanied by the manager of his seafood restaurant on Fisherman's Wharf, his brother Tom and his wife, and an old friend from his days on the minor leagues.

Marilyn signed the marriage certificate as Norma Jeane Mortenson Dougherty and confusingly gave her age as 25.

Despite the secrecy surrounding the wedding, there was a sizable crowd of several hundred people outside City Hall when Joe and Marilyn emerged. Some reporters had gathered and asked, among other things, if the DiMaggios were going to have any children; they both agreed they would – Joe wanted one, Marilyn, six.

From there they headed off on honeymoon. Their first evening was spent in a small town 200 miles south of San Francisco, having dinner followed by a night in a motel. From there the couple went to a friend's mountain lodge above Palm Springs, where they spent two weeks. According to Marilyn there wasn't even a television set, which must have been agony for DiMaggio who by all accounts was addicted. After Joe had briefly flown to New York, he and Marilyn met up again in San Francisco where they took a Pan Am Clipper flight to Tokyo, via Hawaii. Joe was on baseball business; 20th Century-Fox scrapped the idea of *The Girl In Pink Tights*.

Robert Mitchum and Marilyn in *River Of No Return*, 1954

River of No Return (1954)

Making the film that Marilyn's co-star Robert Mitchum dubbed 'the picture of no return' proved to be hard work for all those involved. Marilyn got injured, tempers frayed, and life on location tested everyone's limits. Supposedly set in the Northwestern USA in 1875, widower Matt Calder arrives in town after a jail term to seek out his 10-year-old son, who has been left in the care of saloon singer Kay Weston and her gambler husband. Reclaiming his son, they head off into the wilderness where they later rescue the Westons from their floundering raft, only to have Harry Weston steal Calder's horse and gun and leave his wife, Calder, and son stranded and at the mercy of Indians. After various adventures Calder kills Weston in a fair fight and he and Kay, along with young Mark, live together on the Calder farm.

'There's no doubt that Miss Monroe means every bit of business that she's required to do in the adventure yarn, but the heavily dramatic elements of the film are just a little too much for her at this point in her acting career.' – *Los Angeles Examiner*

The original story on which Frank Fenton based the screenplay was by Louis Lantz, who used *The Bicycle Thief*, an Italian film from 1948, as his inspiration. Fox stalwart Lionel Newman and Ken Darby wrote Marilyn's songs. However, the film was far from Marilyn's best, and she in later years decried it as the worst she ever made. Her relationship with Preminger, as well as his with Fox, helped persuade the 47-year-old director to buy his way out of his 20th Century-Fox contract.

'She tried very hard, and when people try hard, you can't be mad at them.' ~ Otto Preminger in 1980

CAST & CREDITS
Robert Mitchum – Matt Calder
Marilyn Monroe – Kay Weston
Rory Calhoun – Harry Weston
Tommy Rettig – Mark Calder
Murvyn Vye – Dave Colby
Douglas Spencer – Sam Benson

Director – Otto Preminger
Producer – Stanley Rubin
Screenplay – Frank Fenton
Music – Cyril J. Mockridge
Cinematography – Joseph LaShelle
Studio – 20th Century-Fox

PLAYBOY AND THE PLAYGIRL

'There is nothing else quite like Marilyn on this good earth.'
~ The first issue of Playboy

SHORTLY BEFORE MARRYING Joe DiMaggio, Marilyn made a further step toward iconic status when she appeared on the cover of the very first issue of *Playboy* magazine in December 1953. It was not another nude photo shoot for Marilyn, they simply used a picture that had appeared on the infamous calendar, along with another taken in Atlantic City when she had offered a photographer a little too much cleavage for DiMaggio's liking. It's been said that for his wedding present Marilyn gave Joe DiMaggio a set of her nude shots from 1949. Nearly two years later Marilyn would again grace the cover of *Playboy*.

Following on from her Japan trip with her new husband, Marilyn went to Korea two days after Valentine's day 1954 to entertain the troops, many of whom had probably bought *Playboy*. Back from the Far East, Marilyn and Joe stayed at his home in San Francisco where they remained off the gossip columnists' radar for over a month. After returning to Hollywood to rebuild the bridges with 20th Century-Fox, Marilyn and Joe moved in to a rented house on North Palm Drive in Beverly Hills. Marilyn was doing prep work for her next movie, and at the end of April *River of No Return* had its premiere in Denver followed by a first showing in Los Angeles a week later.

The new movie on which Marilyn was working was *There's No Business like Show Business*, which began shooting at the end of May; during filming it began to become clear that all was not well between her and Joe. He was the very antithesis of Hollywood and she could just not get to grips with the older man's lifestyle. On the one occasion he attended the Fox lot during filming, DiMaggio, so frustrated with the whole business, refused to be photographed with Marilyn in what he considered a far-too-revealing costume.

Marilyn was not enjoying filming. Behind-the-scenes contract negotiations involving Charles Feldman and Darryl Zanuck were going slowly and she felt increasingly like a pawn in their game. What particularly irked her was that having agreed to make *There's No Business Like Show Business* at Fox, it now seemed the film that Marilyn really wanted to make — *The Seven Year Itch* with Billy Wilder — was not to be made at the studio; as a contract player it could mean she would lose the opportunity to appear in it. She only agreed to *Show Business* to get *The Itch*. Eventually a deal was done between Fox and Wilder, but even this angered Marilyn as she thought Feldman had somehow compromised her position. By the beginning of August, Marilyn had finished work on *Show Business* and with just a few days' break she was back at work with Billy Wilder. With all the pressure something had to give.

'A wife should see to it that his shoes and suits are sent out to be cleaned.' ~ Marilyn

Marilyn entertains U.S. troops in South Korea, 16 February 1954

LITTLE BITTY PRETTY ONE

'I'm just a pretty girl who's soon forgotten, but not Joe, he's an all-time great.' ~ **Marilyn**

BILLY WILDER was born in a region that is now part of Poland and arrived in Hollywood as a 27-year-old in 1933. In 1946 he won Oscars for both directing and writing the screenplay of *The Lost Weekend,* and then in 1951 he won another for the screenplay of *Sunset Boulevard*. Marilyn was desperate to work with him on *The Seven Year Itch* from the moment she was first told about the project by Feldman.

It was a matter of days after wrapping up work on *There's No Business Like Show Business* that Marilyn flew out of Los Angeles bound for New York's La Guardia airport; Joe DiMaggio was there to send her on her way with a farewell kiss. Marilyn's feet had barely touched the ground before she was filming exterior sequences for *The Seven Year Itch*. One of the shots was the iconic scene of Marilyn in a white dress with her skirt blowing up around her waist while standing over an air duct.

While for us it is an iconic movie moment, it was an apocalyptic moment in Marilyn and Joe's relationship. DiMaggio had arrived in New York a few days before the scene was shot and watched it being filmed; it sent his delicate Italian sensibilities over the precipice. The cast and senior crew were all staying in the St. Regis Hotel on East 55th Street in the heart of Manhattan, and no-one in rooms near to those occupied by Mr and Mrs DiMaggio got much sleep that night.

A few days later the feuding couple flew home to Hollywood; by the first few days of October it became clear to those close to Marilyn that it was over between her and Joe. Cue the 20th Century-Fox publicity machine to craft a carefully stage-managed announcement that highlighted the fact that their careers were in conflict. Meanwhile Marilyn and Joe stayed together in their rented house at 508 Palm Drive, but on Wednesday morning, 6 October, the announcement was made to the phalanx of pressmen waiting outside the couple's Beverly Hill's home. Minutes later DiMaggio sped off in his blue Cadillac and headed home to San Francisco.

Almost an hour later, Marilyn came out of the ranch-style house in a high-necked black jersey dress with her arm on that of Jerry Giesler, the Hollywood lawyer who habitually was there when needed in such circumstances. All that was left was for Marilyn and Joe and their lawyers to sift through the debris of their doomed relationship. The marriage of the Italian-American sports jock and the poor little pretty girl was

'The marriage was a big mistake for Marilyn and I feel she has known it for a long time.'
~ **Natasha Lytess, Marilyn's drama coach**

never going to work. Marilyn was granted a divorce on 27 October 1954. To all intents and purposes their marriage had lasted nine months – there were no children.

A few days after Marilyn finished shooting *The Seven Year Itch* and following a day when she was recording a last song for *There's No Business Like Show Business,* there occurred an incident that was bizarre even by Hollywood standards.

It was on 5 November and involved the other legendary Italian-American of their generation. It's been said that Joe DiMaggio was to baseball what Frank Sinatra was to singing, and few would argue. Sinatra was having his own issues on the marital front. Frank's Marilyn was Ava Gardner and aspects of both relationships were very similar. The story of what happened that night did not surface until almost a year later and when it did, it was courtesy of one of Hollywood's more salacious gossip magazines.

According to the story in *Confidential* in September 1955, Frank and Joe were at Patsy D'Amore's Villa Capri restaurant when Joe got a call from a private detective who had been tailing Marilyn to say she was in an apartment at 754 Kilkea Drive. Joe told the guy "Hold everything till I get there." DiMaggio arrived soon after, accompanied by Sinatra and Billy D'Amore, the husband of the owner of the Villa Capri. "The latter pair were along for the excitement," said *Confidential.* Joe thought his wife was in the apartment of Sheila and Hal Schaefer; Hal was Marilyn's vocal coach who had first worked with her on *Gentlemen Prefer Blondes.* DiMaggio was convinced Marilyn was having an affair with Schaefer (years later Schaefer confirmed they were) and

decided to beak into the apartment where the supposed assignation was taking place. Sinatra's role in this incident is at best unclear or at least clouded in misinformation, but he was very definitely there when DiMaggio broke down the door of the apartment. Marilyn was not inside, just a rather confused and probably very frightened older lady sitting bolt upright in bed, "her nightgown around her ribs and starring in utter terror." If only they had picked the right door!

In fact the apartment that Marilyn was in belonged to an actress named Sheila Stewart, who was there with her, as was Hal Schaefer. Quite why DiMaggio wanted to catch his ex-wife with another man is unclear. Maybe it was bravado, egged on by Sinatra and the other friends he was dining with at the Villa Capri. Whatever the reason it became known as the 'Wrong Door Incident.' Even more bizarrely, Marilyn and Joe began seeing something of each other in the weeks that followed the incident. There was talk of reconciliation, but none occurred.

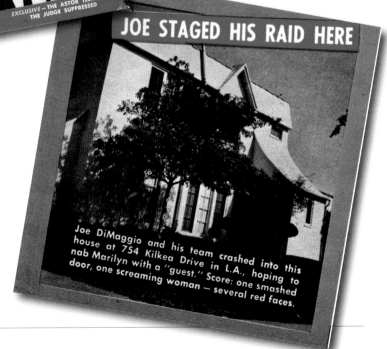

JOE STAGED HIS RAID HERE

Joe DiMaggio and his team crashed into this house at 754 Kilkea Drive in L.A., hoping to nab Marilyn with a "guest." Score: one smashed door, one screaming woman — several red faces.

Mitzi Gaynor, director Walter Lang, Ethel Merman, vocal director Ken Darby, Donald O'Connor, Johnnie Ray, and Marilyn

relax on the set of *There's No Business Like Show Business*, 20th Century-Fox studios, 1954

There's No Business Like Show Business (1954)

The film's title is taken from a song by Irving Berlin featured in *Annie Get Your Gun*; it inspired Lamar Trotti to write a story that then became a screenplay. The movie is based upon the fictional 'Five Donahues', a singing and dancing family, who are at the top of the show-business ladder that Vicky is attempting to climb from the bottom rung. She works as a hat-check girl and falls in love with Tim Donahue, one of Terence and Molly's three grown-up children. It puts pressure on the close-knit family; naturally it all ends happily.

'Miss Gaynor has the jump on Miss Monroe, whose wriggling and squirming to 'Heat Wave' and 'Lazy' are embarrassing to behold.' ~ *New York Times*

The songs are a mish-mash of old Irving Berlin material from a variety of sources that do nothing to help the musical seem contemporary in any way. Seven years later George Chakiris would star in *West Side Story*, but in this film he was an uncredited dancer in one of his first Hollywood appearances. The 'Nabob of Sob,' as Johnnie Ray had been dubbed, was not a great piece of casting other than he was hugely popular with audiences in both America and Britain. He had had his first hit on the *Billboard* charts at the end of 1951 when 'Cry' spent 11 weeks at No.1.

'*There's No Business Like Show Business* is a big extravaganza, colorfully bright and melodic. Just lots of plain, wonderful sentiment.' ~ *New York Daily Mirror*

CAST & CREDITS

Ethel Merman – Molly Donahue
Donald O'Connor – Tim Donahue
Marilyn Monroe – Vicky
Dan Dailey – Terence Donahue
Johnnie Ray – Steve Donahue
Mitzi Gaynor – Katy Donahue

Director – Walter Lang
Producer – Sol C. Siegel
Screenplay – Phoebe Ephron & Henry Ephron
Music – Songs, Irving Berlin, music by Alfred & Lionel Newman, Earle Hagen, Bernard Mayers, Hal Schaefer & Herbert Spencer
Cinematography – Leon Shamroy
Studio – 20th Century-Fox

FAME AND
NO FORTUNE

'I didn't like a lot of my pictures. I'm tired of sex roles. I'm going to broaden my scope.' ~ Marilyn in New York, January 1955

JUST AFTER THE 'Wrong Door Incident' Marilyn did a photo shoot for Muscular Dystrophy in which she looked a long way from her best. The strain of the emotional and professional calls upon her was certainly showing. *There's No Business Like Show Business* had its premiere on 16 December 1954 in New York City. Marilyn had arrived on the East Coast a week or so earlier but did not attend. Having left Hollywood she had fallen out with not just 20th Century-Fox but she had also fired her agent Charles Feldman, as well as her lawyer. She had gone East to stay with Milton Greene and his wife Amy at their 18th-century Connecticut farmhouse.

Milton Greene had met Marilyn when she and DiMaggio were in their courting-but-serious phase. As a photographer he was in Hollywood on an assignment for *Look* magazine. He and Marilyn struck up a real friendship and so when she decided to leave Hollywood and strike out on her own it was with Milton and his wife's support and encouragement. He had looked over her contract and given Marilyn advice on what was wrong with it – there was little right with it, but it was far from unusual for the time.

After a family Christmas in Connecticut, during which Marilyn by all accounts spent much of the time on the telephone fending off famous callers anxious to work with her, or just finding out what was going on, she re-entered the world. She and Milton formed Marilyn Monroe Productions and severed her relationship with 20th Century-Fox. Shortly afterwards, Marilyn moved to a suite in the Waldorf Astoria Towers in Manhattan and lived a lavish lifestyle that was funded by Greene, as she had no money of her own.

Greene worked tirelessly trying to negotiate deals with studios to put a film into production, and part of this strategy was a CBS television program on 8 April 1955. It was filmed at the Greenes' farmhouse with Edward R. Murrow, the broadcaster who had been such an important 'voice to America' from London during the early years of World War II. The ten-minute interview showed Marilyn to be eager to please and relaxed with the Greenes, but she seemed uncertain about exactly where her career and life might be heading.

NEXT WEEK IN PICTUREGOER
...you can read all about a new influence in the life of Marilyn Monroe. After the world's top pin-up girl quarrelled with Fox, there was silence. Suddenly M.M. Productions Inc.—and a new-style Marilyn—emerged. Guy Austin tells the story of
THE MAN BEHIND MONROE

'What do you hope for with Monroe Productions?' asked Ed Murrow. 'To contribute to help making good pictures.' ~ Marilyn on CBS TV's Person to Person, 8 April 1955

Marilyn Monroe surveys the city from a balcony of the Ambassador Hotel, New York City, 1955

The Seven Year Itch (1955)

The film is taken from a play of the same name written by George Axelrod that had opened in New York in 1952. Tom Ewell had played Richard Sherman in the stage production and it's his itch to which the title refers. He sends his wife Helen and their son out of New York to escape the worst of the summer heat and then he meets 'the girl' – a model who is renting the upstairs apartment. After a series of fantastic events in which Sherman tries to convince himself that 'the girl' is not going to get him to waver, which of course she's not trying to do anyway, he eventually flees to join his wife and son in Maine, far away from the irritating heat of the city.

'This is the picture every red-blooded American male has been awaiting ever since the publication of the tease photos showing the wind lifting Marilyn Monroe's skirt above her shapely gams. It was worth waiting for.' ~ *New York Daily Mirror*

The film was substantially rewritten because much of the play's material was considered 'indecent' for cinemagoers. The iconic scene with Marilyn in her white dress was filmed first on New York's Lexington Avenue at 52nd Street and then again back in the Fox studio for the final movie version; the location shooting was used to generate publicity for the film prior to its release.

'The screen adaptation concerns only the fantasies, and omits the acts, of the summer bachelor, who remains totally, if unbelievably, chaste. Morality wins if honesty loses, but let's not get into that.' ~ *Variety*

CAST & CREDITS
Marilyn Monroe – The Girl
Tom Ewell – Richard Sherman
Evelyn Keyes – Helen Sherman
Sonny Tufts – Tom MacKenzie

Director – Billy Wilder
Producers – Charles Feldman & Billy Wilder
Screenplay – Billy Wilder & George Axelrod
Music –Alfred Newman
Cinematography – Milton R Krasner
Studio – 20th Century-Fox

That famous air duct scene in *The Seven Year Itch*

Marilyn arriving at Lee Strasberg's Actors Studio, New York City, 1955

NEW YORK CITY, YOU'RE A WOMAN

'That's the way they think of me, with my skirt over my head.'
~ Marilyn, June 1955

Shortly before her appearance on *Person to Person* Marilyn met Cheryl Crawford who, along with Elia Kazan, was one of the co-founders of the Actors Studio in 1947 as well as a major Broadway producer. By 1951 Lee Strasberg had taken over the running of the Studio. Marilyn told Crawford she was interested in becoming a serious actor and began having private lessons with her. Marilyn soon met Strasberg and his wife Paula and began working at the Studio proper; for his part, Strasberg was captivated by what her saw in her.

The Actors Studio had just moved to its current location in what had been the Seventh Associate Presbyterian Church on New York City's West 44th Street, and it was there that Strasberg took over from Crawford and began schooling Marilyn. She would arrive dressed in casual clothes, without make-up, and as one fellow actor said, she appeared to be able to switch her 'Monroe character' off and on.

Not only was Marilyn working with the Strasbergs but she spent a great deal of time in the New York City home and much less time out at the Greenes' Connecticut farmhouse. She immersed herself in the company of actors, poets, and the Strasbergs' world. She visited art galleries, went to plays and enthusiastically embraced the Manhattan arts scene. It was while she was going through the Actors Studio's sessions that *The Seven Year Itch* had its premiere in New York on 1 June. Eli Wallach, the actor who befriended Marilyn during these acting sessions, remembered being surprised at how she looked at the posters of herself in the white dress with a sense of detachment. There was talk of Marilyn and Joe getting back together, but the more time she spent in New York City with the arts crowd the less likely this became; nevertheless it was DiMaggio who accompanied her to the premiere of *The Seven Year Itch* at Loew's State Theater on her 29th birthday.

Marilyn was invited to many parties with Lee and Paula Strasberg and others she met at the Actors Studio. At these parties she occasionally bumped into people she knew from her Hollywood days; back in April she had met Arthur Miller, who was not a regular on the 'New York scene', preferring to spend time at his home in Connecticut. Shortly after the party he called his friend Paula Strasberg asking if she had a telephone number for Marilyn. Miller arranged to meet Marilyn at the home of Norman Rosten, a poet and old friend from their university days.

The Egghead and the Hourglass were about to become lovers.

The Egghead & the Hourglass

1956–1959

From the almost frenetic movie-making of the first half of the decade, Marilyn slowed to a snail's pace and turned out just one film a year for the second half, although in 1958 she had no movies released. Marilyn married her second husband, a man as different from her first as it's possible to be. Would she at last find happiness?

THE LODESTONE AND THE FREEDOM FIGHTER

'He (Arthur Miller) introduced me to the importance of political freedom in this country.' ~ **Marilyn**

WHEREAS MARILYN'S RELATIONSHIP with DiMaggio was carried on in the full, intense white glare of publicity from the day they first met, Marilyn's relationship with Arthur Miller was, for almost a year, conducted in almost absolute secrecy. Even many of those closest to Marilyn did not know she was seeing Miller in New York.

For Miller, despite having been instantly attracted to Marilyn when they first met in Hollywood in 1951, it was a no easy decision to begin the affair. He married his high school sweetheart in 1940 and the couple had two children, but their marriage, for all sorts of reasons, had got stuck in the doldrums. Nevertheless, Miller, as cerebral as DiMaggio was physical, struggled with his conscience. His work was so important to him and following on from the success of Death of A Salesman his play about the Salem witch trials, The Crucible, opened in 1953, yet it failed to live up to his, or other people's, expectations. Miller's stance on the McCarthy witch hunt was reflected in The Crucible and his failure to testify placed him at odds with the U.S. Government – he was refused a passport in 1954 when he wanted to attend the Belgian opening of The Crucible.

Despite their secret meetings, or perhaps because of them,

Marilyn also saw other men during the second half of 1955. Besides DiMaggio accompanying her to the premiere of The Seven Year Itch she had a brief affair with Marlon Brando and there were, by all accounts, other men. On 29 September 1955 Marilyn attended the first night of Miller's new play, A View From The Bridge, but was careful to avoid meeting the playwright and his wife by sitting on the opposite side of the auditorium of the Coronet Theater on West 49th Street (It's now the Eugene O'Neill Theater).

Marilyn was still living in the three-room apartment on the 27th floor of the Waldorf Astoria Towers in Manhattan, and by this time MCA, the influential Hollywood agency, was in discussions with 20th Century-Fox following her suspension by the studio. MCA were endeavoring to secure Marilyn some extra payments for her recent films, as well as trying to negotiate a new and better contract. There were also protracted discussions involving the British playwright Terence Rattigan and the notorious British theatrical entrepreneur Binkie Beaumont over Marilyn appearing in The Sleeping Prince. Having not worked for over a year Marilyn certainly needed the money; the production company she formed with Milton Greene had so far been a financial non-starter.

'She's (Marilyn Monroe) kind of a lodestone that draws out of the male animal his essential qualities.' ~ **Arthur Miller**

Playwright Arthur Miller in the workshop he built at his home in Connecticut, 1954

NEXT STOP – HOLLYWOOD

'Laurence Olivier is said to be 'tickled pink' to be starring in a film with Marilyn.' ~ **Daily Mirror, 1 January 1956**

AS 1955 WAS COMING TO AN END Marilyn conducted a number of in-depth interviews, including one with British newspaper the Daily Mirror. She spoke candidly about her upbringing and her life in Hollywood. Besides talking to Marilyn the paper tracked down Tom Kelley, who had photographed Marilyn for the calendar. He revealed that he paid her $50 and that he played an Artie Shaw record while Marilyn posed naked. "I find 'Begin the Beguine' helps to create vibrations." Let's hope they were good ones. Marilyn also spoke with Earl Wilson, the famed New York columnist and reporter, who was far more clued into what was going on in her life in Manhattan than the British newspaper. Wilson got an admission from Marilyn that her favorite playwright was Arthur Miller, but she quickly added that she also admired Tennessee Williams.

Marilyn's continuing work at the Actors Studio culminated in her performing a scene from Eugene O'Neill's Anna Christie, which by all accounts was a major trial as she struggled to remember her lines. Perhaps it was because Marilyn had business on her mind. As the year ended she signed once again for 20th Century-Fox, although it was on vastly different terms than her previous contract with the studio. She was only required to make four films in seven years; through her production company she would receive well over a million dollars in annual salary when measured in today's money. On top of that Marilyn could make one movie

each year for another studio and she was also guaranteed a share of her movies' profits. In all, she could expect to get somewhere near $100 million (in today's money) for seven years' work.

A day after the deal was inked Fox announced that rather than The Sleeping Prince, Marilyn's first film for Fox was to be Bus Stop, directed by Joshua Logan for Marilyn Monroe Productions and 20th Century-Fox. Milton Greene announced that Marilyn was in negotiations to make The Sleeping Prince after Bus Stop, and her co-star was to be Sir Laurence Olivier, Vivian Leigh's husband and one of Britain's foremost actors. The press naturally made mention of what had happened, but their entertainment pages were dominated by the news that Grace Kelly was to marry Prince Rainier of Monaco; even Marilyn couldn't compete with that.

On 9 February Marilyn and Larry, as he insisted everyone call him, attended a press conference in New York at which Olivier saw Marilyn-mania at close quarters as photographers jostled each other for prime position. Marilyn, in a low-cut black velvet dress and jacket, had a wardrobe malfunction when the strap of her dress broke, and this very nearly caused a photographers' stampede. Olivier was to experience Marilyn-mania of another kind at even closer quarters when the two of them got down to filming later in the year.

At the press conference, Marilyn proved herself to be a not inconsiderable actress when she was asked if there was any romance in her life at present. "No, I wish there were." Olivier, for his part, flirtatiously added, "You don't wish anything of the sort." However, romance was very much on Marilyn's mind; a few weeks earlier Earl Wilson had announced that the 40-year-old Arthur Miller and his wife were to get a divorce.

From New York Marilyn flew to Hollywood; it was the first time she had been there since leaving to live on the East Coast the previous year. It was a very different Marilyn from the one that had left. She was now more confident, a better actress, and she had Milton Greene by her side. It had been Greene who had suggested Logan as director of Bus Stop, and Marilyn's partner worked hard to ensure that the asset in which he owned an almost half share was treated well. Not that he had anything to worry about. Strasberg had told Logan what a good actress Marilyn had become, and after his initial trepidation about working with her he found she was delightful.

Logan's only real problem was the fact that Marilyn had hired Paula Strasberg as her acting coach. Strasberg was permanently on set and she was no easy person to get along with; her own daughter described her as a "combination of delicatessen, pharmacist, and Jewish mother." She naturally used the 'method acting' approach made famous

by Lee Strasberg which some who were working on the film found ridiculous – this was Hollywood not Broadway. Logan, though, was very supportive of Marilyn throughout, becoming a co-conspirator on many of the ideas that Marilyn and he dreamed up.

During the making of Bus Stop Marilyn appeared on the cover of Time magazine, proof of her collateral as well as wonderful news for Fox and the movie. Everything seemed to be going right for Marilyn, including her love life. Arthur Miller, having separated from his wife, headed to Reno while Marilyn was filming in Hollywood. He stayed there for six weeks in order to qualify under Nevada's arcane laws that allowed for 'quickie' divorces. Marilyn and Miller would speak on the phone every day while he stayed at a guest ranch north of Reno.

As soon as Bus Stop was finished in early June, Marilyn went to New York to meet up with Miller who was due to follow a week or so later. Everything was set, both were free to marry and they planned to honeymoon in England so that Marilyn could work with Olivier.

However, there was one small problem for Miller. The specter of communism and his involvement with fellow-travelers was about to raise its head again.

'America's best known moving picture star is now the darling of the left-wing intelligentsia; several of whom are listed as red-fronters. I do not think she realizes it.'
~ **Columnist Walter Winchell, from FBI files**

Marilyn and Don Murray in *Bus Stop*, 1956

Bus Stop (1956)

The original Broadway production of *Bus Stop*, written by William Inge, opened at the Music Box Theater and ran for 478 performances. It's the story of Bo, a naive and unworldly rodeo cowboy, and his friend Virgil. Bo falls in love with Cherie, a singer in Phoenix, and wants to take her to Montana but Cherie wants Hollywood. After scuffles, arguments and the likelihood of Bo losing Cherie, she relents and decides to go with him to live happily in the wilds of Montana. This drama is not something that many would have picked as Marilyn's movie comeback. Her time in New York learning to be an actor and the influence of those around her clearly played a part in her decision.

'Marilyn Monroe has finally proved herself an actress in *Bus Stop*.' ~ *New York Times*

Joshua Logan was 48-years-old when he directed *Bus Stop*; he later directed a number of movie musicals – *South Pacific* (1958), *Camelot* (1967) and *Paint Your Wagon* (1969). Despite *Bus Stop* not being a musical, Marilyn sings 'That Old Black Magic' to establish her credentials as a singer. Don Murray was nominated for an Oscar and Marilyn for a Golden Globe for Best Actress in a Comedy or Musical… it's a strange nomination as *Bus Stop* is neither.

'In *Bus Stop* Marilyn Monroe effectively dispels once and for all the notion that she is merely a glamour personality.' ~ *The Saturday Review*

CAST & CREDITS
Marilyn Monroe – Cherie
Don Murray – Beauregard 'Bo' Decker
Arthur O'Connell – Virgil Blessing
Betty Field – Grace
Hope Lange – Elma Duckworth
Eileen Heckart – Vera

Director – Joshua Logan
Producer – Buddy Adler
Screenplay – George Axelrod
Music – Alfred Newman & Cyril Mockridge
Cinematography – Milton Krasner
Studio – 20th Century-Fox & Marilyn Monroe Productions

REDS IN BED

'I will be there to be with the woman who will then be my wife.'
~ Arthur Miller, when asked at the HUAC hearing why he wanted to go to England, 21 June 1956

AS MILLER WAS preparing to leave Nevada he was subpoenaed to appear before the House Un-American Activities Committee. Miller had no intention of naming names and he didn't. Ironically there were those who wanted Marilyn to end her relationship with Miller "for the good of her career." But instead she supported him totally, both then and over the next couple of years as she paid some of Miller's legal costs.

Miller's admission that he was going to marry was the prelude to pandemonium; Marilyn's apartment was put under virtual siege. Over the next few days there was frantic planning by the couple; a press conference was set for 29 June. En route to the press call, and while driving at some speed, Miller and Marilyn were followed by two journalists. The driver in the pursuing car lost control and crashed, his passenger, who was head of the local Paris-Match office, was thrown through the windshield. Miller and Marilyn stopped and rushed back on foot to drag the two people from the wreckage; it was a horrific sight that no one would want to witness. They then drove on ahead and called for an ambulance but Maria Scherbatoff, who had gone through the windshield, died on the operating table.

Although they were both terribly shocked by what had occurred, the couple decided to marry that evening; going before a judge in the Westchester County Court House in White Plains, New York they were pronounced man and wife at 7:21pm. Two days later they had a Jewish wedding at the house in Katonah, New York before heading to Miller's farmhouse in Roxbury, Connecticut.

Before and after the wedding there was intense, behind-the-scenes wrangling over Miller's HUAC appearance. It seemed likely that the House of Representatives would cite Miller for contempt and he would have his passport confiscated. Spyros Skouras, who was running 20th Century-Fox, having eased Darryl F. Zanuck out, would do nothing to support Miller, despite pleading from Marilyn and her advisors. Such was the level of hysteria, there were even accusations in FBI files that Marilyn Monroe Productions had entered the Communist Party's orbit. Finally, Miller was given permission to travel.

Marilyn, dressed in a tight sweater and pencil skirt, and Arthur Miller left New York's Idlewild Airport on Friday 13 July on a Trans World Airlines flight to London so that she could begin shooting The Sleeping Prince. At London Airport, Laurence Olivier and Vivien Leigh were there to meet them and together they held an impromptu press conference.

'A to M, June 1956. Now is forever.'
~ The words inscribed inside Marilyn's wedding band

Marilyn waves to the press and her fans at the Savoy Hotel, London, 15 July 1956

MRS MILLER

'He calls her Mrs Miller and dares you to call her anything else.' ~ Daily Mirror, 16 July 1956

THE MILLERS WENT straight from the airport to Parkside House in sleepy Englefield Green, where Olivier had organized a house for them to rent while Marilyn was filming at Pinewood Studios. It was near Windsor Great Park, so Marilyn and Miller were spotted on a number of occasions bike-riding through the royal park that surrounds Windsor Castle. The beautiful house belonged to Baron Moore of Cobham; Marilyn had a former Scotland Yard detective as a bodyguard, a chauffer and a Portuguese couple as cook and butler.

The following day, the Millers were driven into central London for a more formal press conference at the Savoy Hotel. Marilyn felt that Olivier's aloofness, as she perceived it, was a rebuff, whereas Olivier was simply acting professionally in front of the press; it was the beginning of an uneasy working relationship between the two of them. The situation was not helped by Olivier being none too enamored by Arthur Miller – he disliked his plays and found him smug. Added to which, Olivier was not just Marilyn's co-star he was also her director. It was not long before Miller felt dislike for Olivier; he reflected his wife's unhappiness as well as something of an old-fashioned attitude in coping with his

The Millers at Parkside House, Englefield Green, England, July 1956

wife working at all.

Before shooting even started, Marilyn was in a bad mood. She found out that her favorite scene had been cut from Bus Stop; not by its director, but by Fox. Could she trust Olivier who had seemed so perfect when they were in New York, but who now seemed so distant? The first day of test filming went badly, with Marilyn wanting reassurance while Olivier craved professionalism and progress. Nevertheless, when Olivier looked at the first day's rushes he saw why Marilyn was a star – the camera loved her. Rehearsals were due to begin a week later before shooting proper began in August. Before the rehearsals began, Miller heard that Congress had voted overwhelmingly for him to be cited for contempt; it put a damper on their honeymoon and contributed to Marilyn feeling unhappy with everything.

Paula Strasberg had come to London with Marilyn, which upset Olivier no end; as filming went on he found it almost intolerable. Strasberg acted as the conduit for Olivier's directorial instructions, causing the whole thing to descend into bad-tempered farce. It was no way to make a movie.

Vivien Leigh, Sir Laurence Olivier, Marilyn, and Arthur Miller, England, July 1956

THERE'S METHOD
IN THE MADNESS

'She probably knows more about acting in films than anyone in the world.' ~ **Joshua Logan to Sir Laurence Olivier**

VERY EARLY DURING filming Olivier managed to upset his co-star by asking her to be 'sexy Marilyn Monroe.' She interpreted this as insinuating that she couldn't act and was some kind of one-dimensional puppet. For his part, all Olivier wanted was to see the woman in the test film. For her part, Marilyn became so befuddled with Strasberg's method acting instructions that she had stopped being Marilyn.

Back at Parkside, Miller was busy working on rewrites for A View From The Bridge that was to open in October. As Marilyn's anxieties over her film grew he became increasingly frustrated with his own work. Tensions increased by the day. Olivier had his own off-set issues when Vivien Leigh miscarried their child. Leigh, who was a manic-depressive, sunk into the depths of despair, which naturally reflected on Olivier's ability to remain calm under the mayhem of working with Marilyn and her retinue.

Then came the worst blow of all. After a couple of weeks of filming, Marilyn and Miller had a vicious argument; Marilyn was distraught because he would not, unconditionally, take her side against what she saw as the conspiracy against her by everyone who did not work for Marilyn Monroe Productions. The Millers had been married barely two months when Arthur decided to fly home to America. When he had left, Marilyn found out she was pregnant; days later she miscarried.

Frustrated in her work, Marilyn took increasingly to drugs, which only made everything worse. She thought Olivier was trying to sabotage her movie and, with Paula Strasberg whispering in her ear, Marilyn, her director and co-star were openly at war on set. Then to cap it all, Lee Strasberg arrived. Olivier simply refused him admission to Pinewood studios and the impasse continued.

When Miller returned, his play opened on Thursday 11 October. The Oliviers were there and Mrs Miller looked stunning in an off-the-shoulder red satin evening gown – she was the Marilyn Monroe that her director wanted her to be, but was unable to get her to perform. Back at Pinewood, filming went on but it was a continual drama and it was a miracle that the film was completed. The Millers left on 20 November; their honeymoon had turned into a nightmare, one from which their marriage would never fully recover. As one newspaper reported the following day, "The wiggle has now disappeared amid a vague miasma of stories about her being late on the set, about her having her hair done at ridiculous hours, about her keeping Larry waiting and making every Tom, Dick and Harry connected with the business hopping mad because of her silly, selfish tantrums."

'I didn't manage to get any of your fish and chips.'
~ Marilyn to reporters at London Airport when asked her biggest disappointment

The Prince and the Showgirl
(1957)

What baffled Olivier from the outset was the fact that Marilyn, whose company owned the rights to Rattigan's *The Sleeping Prince*, acted throughout as if she was working for someone else. It perhaps emphasizes how Marilyn was out of her depth. Working with someone of Olivier's stature would have been difficult for almost any actor, for Marilyn it was impossible. It was some kind of a miracle that it even got finished. It was even more of a miracle that this film about a stuffy prince and a clumsy American who weave a far-fetched tale of political and romantic intrigue did not get panned by the critics.

'Miss Monroe mainly has to giggle, wiggle, breathe deeply and flirt. She does not make the showgirl a person, simply another of her pretty oddities.'
~ *New York Times*

It was Warner Bros. who decided to change the film's name in an attempt to boost ticket sales. Anxious to see the film a success, a photographic session for Olivier and Marilyn was arranged by Milton Greene in New York. Olivier dreaded seeing Marilyn again but against all the odds the photoshoot went brilliantly, far better than any of the filming. The shot used on the movie posters of Olivier kissing Marilyn's shoulder is not in the film, as the *New York Times* were quick to point out in their review on 14 June 1957.

'Marilyn Monroe has never seemed more in command of herself as a person and as a comedienne.' ~ *New York Post*

CAST & CREDITS
Marilyn Monroe – Elsie Marina
Sir Laurence Olivier – Charles, the Prince Regent
Sybil Thorndyke – The Queen Dowager
Richard Wattis – Northbrook

Director – Sir Laurence Olivier
Producer – Sir Laurence Olivier, with Milton Greene & Anthony Bushell
Screenplay – Terence Rattigan
Music – Richard Adinsell
Cinematography – Jack Cardiff
Studio – Warner Bros. Pictures & Marilyn Monroe Productions

Marilyn puts on a cheerful face as she and Miller leave Doctor's Hospital, New York after her miscarriage, 10 August 1957

LIFE WITH THE MILLERS

'Movies are my business, but Arthur is my life.'
~ Marilyn, in an interview in 1957

BACK FROM ENGLAND, the Millers went to Jamaica for a real honeymoon and then moved into an apartment on East 57th Street in Manhattan. All the troubles of England appeared to evaporate and Marilyn seemed blissfully happy with her husband. Years earlier, on Joe DiMaggio's advice, Marilyn had bought the screen rights to Horns of the Devil, a story by Lou Breslow. She sold them to 20th Century-Fox and received $75,000, which allowed her the freedom not to work for a year.

Miller was not so happy with the arrangements concerning Marilyn Monroe Productions. Milton Greene was soon eased out of the company. Arthur Miller did not like him, which sealed his fate; there were even rumors that Greene and Marilyn were lovers. As one newspaper reported, "One thing is proved. Marilyn has a mind of her own. Even if it's on loan from her husband."

When The Prince and The Showgirl came out in June, to better reviews than anyone who had worked on it imagined possible, the Millers were in Connecticut, but made their way to the New York premiere. What no-one knew, apart from their inner circle, was that Marilyn was again pregnant. Two months later she again miscarried, although this time the pregnancy was ectopic and the fetus had to be removed in an operation. By the end of the year the couple, perhaps in their own way trying to get over their sadness, began looking for a new, larger property in Connecticut. They found a 300-acre farm, also near Roxbury, but Marilyn found less solace in the farm than her husband. Her earlier happiness ebbed away as she took far too many sleeping tablets and on at least one occasion her stomach had to be pumped to save her life. She was also drinking way to much for her own good, a habit that had grown out of control while filming in England.

Come late July 1958, Marilyn was on her way back to Hollywood. She had been away for two years and the Hollywood press corps was out in force to record her return. She took a suite in the Bel-Air Hotel and returned to work on 4 August with Billy Wilder on Some Like It Hot, a movie that was for more befitting her talents. However, it was to prove to be a very mixed blessing.

'She's scared and unsure of herself. I found myself wishing that I were a psychoanalyst and she were my patient. It might be that I couldn't have helped her, but she would have looked lovely on a couch.' ~ Billy Wilder

HOT STUFF

'My feeling about Arthur Miller was that he was a little too resentful of his wife.' ~ **Billy Wilder**

BILLY WILDER NEEDED all his directorial skills to work with Marilyn on Some Like It Hot; he also needed stamina as it took five months to complete the picture. Her co-stars were Tony Curtis and Jack Lemmon. The 33-year-old Curtis was one of Hollywood's most popular and busiest actors, having made 13 movies in the three years before he co-starred with Marilyn. A few months older than Curtis, Lemmon would become one of Wilder's favorite actors to work with. Neither her co-stars nor her director could have begun to imagine just how challenging a movie it was going to be – one that has passed into screen legend due to Marilyn's inability to learn her lines. One scene with three words from Marilyn is said to have needed 65 takes.

Marilyn was also unwell. Her state of mind needed constant attention from her psychiatrist, who had been flown in from New York. She also went to hospital several times during filming, as she was once again pregnant. Yet again Marilyn suffered a miscarriage.

Marilyn's marriage was more than a little shaky during her work on Some Like it Hot. There are reports of Miller joining her in Hollywood but not enjoying the experience one little bit. In an exchange with Billy Wilder, Miller expressed

surprise that Marilyn was not arriving until well after lunch for her first shot, as her director pointed out. She had apparently been leaving their room at the Bel-Air around 7:00am.

Tony Curtis was married to Janet Leigh when he made Some Like It Hot, and shortly after he finished the film he was asked what it was like to kiss Marilyn. His answer has passed into movie legend: "It was like kissing Hitler." Recently he has said it was a joke. "It was such a darn stupid question, so I gave a stupid answer." He also confirmed that he and Marilyn had an affair some years before making Some Like It Hot. He has also said that they rekindled their relationship during its making. What's even more surprising is that they admitted their affair to Arthur Miller in Marilyn's dressing room at the studio on N. Formosa Avenue in Hollywood. "I just stood there. The room was so silent that I could hear tyres screeching on Santa Monica Boulevard," said Curtis. Marilyn then told both men that she was pregnant. When Curtis asked Miller what he should do, Marilyn's husband replied. "Finish the film and stay out of our lives." As Marilyn sat there crying, Curtis left her dressing room, walked back to his, and locked the door. It may have accounted for Marilyn's missing mornings.

Thirty-three-year-old heart throb Tony Curtis, 1957

Some Like It Hot (1959)

Adapted from a story by Robert Thoeren and Michael Logan that had originally been made as a German film in 1951. However, some of the scenes were very different. It concerns two musicians who think they witness a mob massacre and so decide to leave town in a hurry by joining an all-girl band. The only problem is that Joe and Jerry are men, so they have to take up cross-dressing. Joe falls in love with Sugar Kane but cannot reveal himself, so he disguises himself as a millionaire named Junior. Through its many scenes and the characters' adventures this wonderful film provides all three leading actors with the best comedic roles of their careers.

'To get down to cases, Marilyn does herself proud, giving a performance of such intrinsic quality that you begin to believe she's only being herself and it is herself who fits into that distant period and this picture so well.' ~ *New York Post*

Originally planned as a color film, it was deemed to be better shot in black-and-white because of the heavy make-up required by Lemmon and Curtis. Costing close to $3 million, it took its title from a line in a child's nursery rhyme. The film's Florida sequence was shot in Coronado, Southern California. In 1972 a stage adaptation was a Broadway hit, and 20 years later it opened in London starring veteran British rock'n'roller Tommy Steele.

'She's [Marilyn] a comedienne with that combination of sex appeal and timing that just can't be beat.' ~ *Variety*

CAST & CREDITS
Marilyn Monroe – Sugar Kane Kowalczyk
Tony Curtis – Joe (Josephine & Junior)
Jack Lemmon – Jerry (Daphne)
George Raft – Spats Colombo
Pat O'Brien – Detective Mulligan

Director – Billy Wilder
Producer – Billy Wilder with I.A.L. Diamond & Doane Harrison
Screenplay – Billy Wilder & I.A.L. Diamond
Music – Adolph Deutsch
Cinematography – Charles Lang
Studio – United Artists

Marilyn and Jack Lemmon on the set of *Some Like It Hot* in Coronado, Southern California, 1958

Soviet Premier Nikita Krushchev chats with Shirley MacLaine on the set of *Can-Can*. Frank Sinatra looks on, September 1959

MARILYN AND THE COMMUNIST

'At first, Marilyn, who never read the papers or listened to the news, had to be told who Khrushchev was.'
~ **Lena Pepitone, Marilyn's maid**

SHOOTING ON Some Like It Hot was completed in November, and soon afterwards Marilyn returned to New York where she entered hospital for some surgery connected with her miscarriages. The Millers spent time out at the 300-acre Roxbury farm, which Arthur found to be the best place to write. Both in Manhattan and Connecticut they entertained friends while on the surface appearing to be blissfully happy.

In reality their marriage was showing increasing signs of strain. Having got Marilyn away from the temptations of Hollywood and the film set, Arthur Miller instead became increasingly fed up with what he saw as the undue influence of the Strasbergs. Following the premiere of Some Like It Hot in March, Marilyn had gone back to work at the Actors Studio, spending increasing time in the city rather than out at their farm. People have talked of Miller appearing detached from Marilyn, others about how badly she treated him – she the star to Miller's tortured writer.

As if to draw attention to their plight, Miller did an interview in the latter part of 1959 that appeared in Esquire magazine under the headline 'The Creative Agony of Arthur Miller'. They could just as well have left out 'creative,' although he was clearly not finding his writing was flowing as it had done previously. There were no new plays, just sheafs of notes.

Given Arthur's brush with Congress and the furore surrounding the HUAC hearings it was perhaps none too surprising that he did not go with Marilyn to Hollywood to meet with the Soviet Premier Khrushchev in September 1959. No doubt few in Congress saw any irony in the Communist leader visiting 20th Century-Fox's studio for a special showing of their movie musical, Can-Can; although Ronald Reagan turned down an invitation to the meet-and-greet. Marilyn decided to wear her tightest, sexiest dress as she considered there probably was not enough sex in the Soviet Union.

Spyros Skouras, the head of Fox, introduced Marilyn to the Premier, who had seen a clip from Some Like It Hot at an American exhibition in Moscow. "You're a very lovely young lady," said Khrushchev, smiling. Marilyn apparently told him she was married and later revealed that "He looked at me the way a man looks on a woman."

'My husband, Arthur Miller, sends you his greetings. There should be more of this kind of thing. It would help both our countries understand each other.' ~ **Marilyn to Khrushchev**

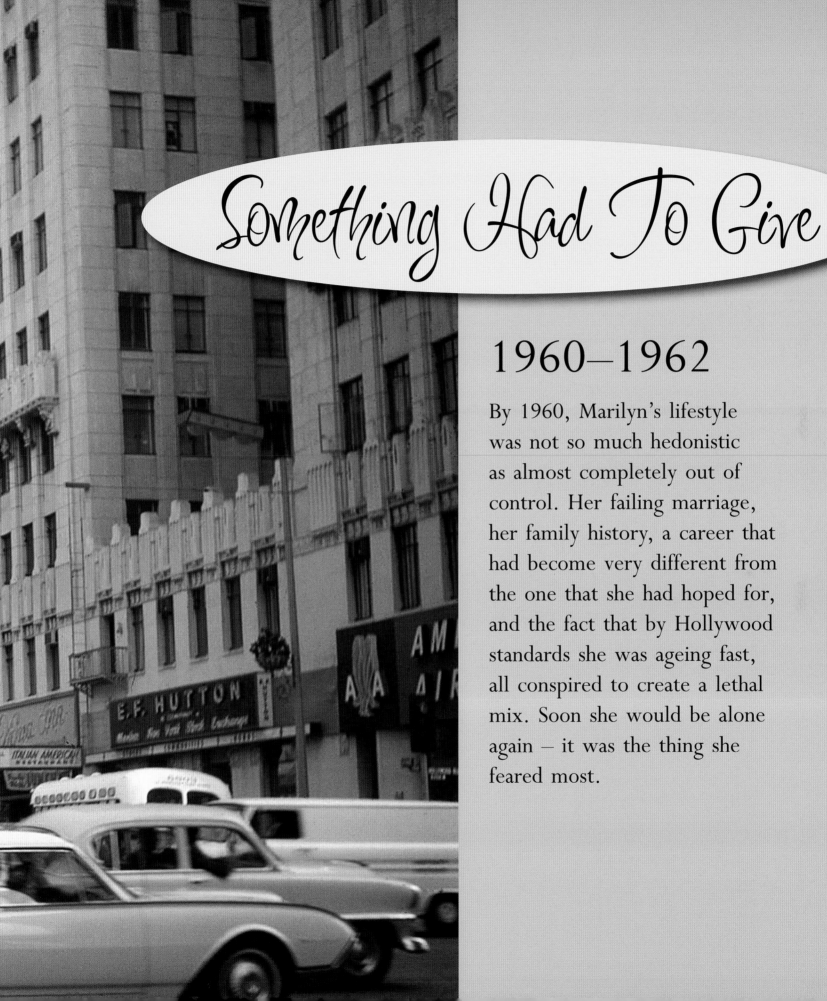

Something Had To Give

1960–1962

By 1960, Marilyn's lifestyle was not so much hedonistic as almost completely out of control. Her failing marriage, her family history, a career that had become very different from the one that she had hoped for, and the fact that by Hollywood standards she was ageing fast, all conspired to create a lethal mix. Soon she would be alone again – it was the thing she feared most.

A CHILD'S AFFAIR

'I've never met anyone quite like Marilyn Monroe, but she is still a child. I'm sorry, but nothing will break up my marriage'
~ Yves Montand

DURING THE SUMMER and fall of 1959, the list of leading men who turned down the chance to appear opposite Marilyn in her next film grew ever longer. It was beginning to read like a Hollywood Who's Who. Some may have had a good reason, others heard that she was not easy to work with. 20th Century-Fox were anxious to get Marilyn back to work as she had so far failed to live up to their expectations, with the exception of *Some Like it Hot*, which had done good business in America and was beginning to open around the world. Eventually Yves Montand, a 38-year-old French singer and film star who had been born in Italy, was cast to appear opposite Marilyn in *Let's Make Love*.

Montand had appeared in the French version of *The Crucible*, and Arthur Miller knew him. MIller very much approved of him playing opposite Marilyn because Montand was a good actor, and also because he and his wife, the actress Simone Signoret, were, to use the phrase popular with the FBI, 'fellow-travelers' to the liberal-leaning Miller.

When filming began in January, both the Millers and the Montands stayed at the Beverly Hills Hotel, spending time together socially as well as professionally. Just like many of Marilyn's recent co-stars, Montand found her difficult as well as annoying to work with. As usual, being late on set was Marilyn's *modus operandi*, but there were days when she did not turn up at all. Things got worse when Arthur left and went back East before flying to Ireland to talk to John Huston about directing a movie that Miller had written. Signoret had also gone home to France, to make a new film, leaving Marilyn in Hollywood where she and Montand began an affair. It soon became the stuff of gossip columns and it was amazing that the Montands' marriage did not end there and then; perhaps it was because they were French.

Montand's remarks about Marilyn being just a child are interesting – he was only five years older than her. Her lack of responsibility, both in her private life and at work, was something Marilyn constantly struggled with. Montand experienced this in all kinds of ways. A few months later, in March 1960, 'the child' won the Golden Globe for Best Actress in Musical or Comedy for her fabulous performance in *Some Like It Hot*. The fact that she had been overlooked for an Oscar was a travesty.

'She's gone without ever knowing that I never stopped wearing the champagne-colored silk scarf she lent me one day.'
~ Simone Signoret

Marilyn and Yves Montand on the set of *Let's Make Love*, 1960

MISFITS

'(It's) now about as funny as pushing grandma down the stairs in a wheelchair.' ~ Gregory Peck speaking about the script for Let's Make Love

THROUGHOUT THE MAKING of *Let's Make Love* Marilyn was seeing a new Hollywood psychiatrist who had long sessions with her at which he tried to keep her head straight about not just her life, but also her role in her new film which she was none too enamored with. Paula Strasberg had been removed from Marilyn's orbit and so there was no-one close to her with whom she was able to discuss her acting. All the signs point to the fact that Marilyn began to feel increasingly

adrift during this period, and this was someone who had never felt firmly anchored At the same time, Marilyn continued taking prescription drugs that were given to her all too readily by doctors who ought to have known better; in Hollywood there has never been a shortage of such doctors.

As work on *Let's Make Love* was nearing the scheduled date for its completion there was doubt that what Marilyn had shot would be enough to produce a finished film. She was emotionally detached from the film as well as being physically absent all too often. She also managed to annoy just about everyone involved in its making. George Cukor, its director, on at least one occasion reduced Marilyn to tears in front of the entire cast and crew.

When filming finally wrapped up a month later, progress on Marilyn's next movie was gathering pace. Work had started on getting cast and director in place well before *Let's Make Love* had even begun shooting. Her next movie was to be the very first film written by Arthur Miller and was to be produced by United Artists. It was also to reunite Marilyn with John Huston, who had directed *The Asphalt Jungle* ten years earlier and had himself been absent from Hollywood for some years. Arthur Miller's story dated from early in their marriage, and its genesis from even earlier. Ironically it concerned divorce and rejection but ultimately happiness.

With the filming of *Let's Make Love* finishing so late, it was just a matter of weeks until work on *The Misfits* was to begin. Most actors need a time to rest and realign themselves between major roles and with Marilyn's problems, and the parlous state of her mind coupled with her drug taking, it was never going to be easy. John Huston, who was unaware of marital difficulties between Arthur and Marilyn, flew into New York from Ireland for meetings with Miller. Meanwhile, Miller was trying desperately to salvage their marriage after Marilyn's unfaithfulness and his feelings of rejection. With just about everyone in Hollywood completely in the know about Marilyn and Montand's affair, it was all so humiliating. There were doubts as to whether it would be possible for *The Misfits* to even begin filming on location in Reno, Nevada. The irony for Miller of it being in Reno, the place that four years earlier he had waited to get his divorce so he could marry Marilyn, could not have been lost on him.

Naturally Huston heard all about Marilyn and Miller's difficulties as soon as colleagues from Hollywood arrived in Reno. He reassured himself with the fact that as Arthur Miller

168

was comfortable about going ahead with the filming then everything would be fine. His only issue was Marilyn's need to be back in Hollywood in mid-July to do some over-dubbing on *Let's Make Love*. Prior to starting the film, Marilyn spent two weeks on the East Coast and all concerned hoped that the equilibrium of being back with her husband and at home in Manhattan and Connecticut would help to focus her.

'Her eyes would be kind of dull.'
~ Tony Randall, a co-star on Let's Make Love

Let's Make Love (1960)

Originally to be called *The Billionaire*, it concerns the wealthy man in question – Jean-Marc Clement – who goes to see the rehearsal of an off-Broadway production in which he is to be satirized. Arriving at the theater, he is mistaken for an actor by the director who asks him to play the character who is to portray the billionaire. Clement readily agrees because he wants to see more of Amanda Dell. Love is all too soon in the air.

'The old Monroe dynamism is lacking in the things she is given to do by the cliché-clogged script.'
~ *The New York Times*

The film featured a number of stars playing themselves – Bing Crosby, Gene Kelly, Milton Berle, and the 'King of the Surf Guitar', Dick Dale as an Elvis Presley impersonator. Despite Marilyn personally asking Frank Sinatra to appear, he refused. Gregory Peck was originally cast opposite Marilyn, but he left the film before shooting began because he was unhappy with the prominence given to her rather than to him. Liverpool-born Frankie Vaughan had a string of British hit singles in the 1950s including a U.K. No.1 with 'Garden of Eden'.

'Monroe, of course, is a sheer delight in the tailor-made role of an off-Broadway actress who wants to better herself intellectually (she is going to night school to study geography), but she also has a uniquely talented co-star in Yves Montand.'
~ *Variety*

CAST & CREDITS
Marilyn Monroe – Amanda Dell
Yves Montand – Jean-Marc Clement /
Alexander Dumas
Tony Randall – Alexander Coffman
Frankie Vaughan – Tony Danton
Wilfrid Hyde-White – George Welch

Director – George Cukor
Producer – Jerry Wald
Screenplay – Norman Krasna
Music – Lionel Newman
Cinematography – Daniel L. Fapp
Studio – 20th Century-Fox

John Huston, Marilyn, and Arthur Miller on the set of *The Misfits*, Reno, Nevada, 1960

LONG LASTING IRONY

'If she goes on at the rate she's going she'll be in an institution in two or three years, or dead.'
~ John Huston, director of The Misfits

A FEW WEEKS AFTER Marilyn began work on *The Misfits*, *Let's Make Love* had its premiere, by which time her new co-star was finding their working relationship intolerable. The former 'King of Hollywood,' Clark Gable, called her "unprofessional" and would get irritated on set waiting for her to show up. Filming at the best of times, when everything goes according to plan, can, with long periods of inactivity be boring, but when you have a star who keeps everyone waiting for so long then nerves become frayed. For Marilyn it was no longer nerves over her acting that was getting the better of her – it was more booze and more pills. Staying at the Mapes Hotel in Reno she was taking up to 20 barbiturates a day washed down with hard liquor. She was frequently comatose in the mornings.

This was when it become completely apparent to everyone involved with *The Misfits* that the Millers had little chance of resurrecting their marriage. Marilyn got to the point of ignoring Arthur in front of people on set and, according to Huston, she "embarrassed him." Things were so bad that she again talked of suicide. Filming in the searing heat of the desert was scarcely bearable for all concerned, but it was Marilyn's state of mind that put her close to the edge. One day she took too many pills, maybe deliberately, or maybe because she was too out of it to know what she was doing. After having her stomach pumped she was flown to Los Angeles and spent ten days in hospital. It was a stay accompanied by the soundtrack of the gossip columnists' typewriters, which did not spare the Millers' dignity. Reporters converged on Nevada to see for themselves what would happen when Marilyn returned to the set.

Miller celebrated his 45th birthday during the making of *The Misfits*, but Marilyn refused to sing 'Happy Birthday' during his party. A month later, when they flew home to New York, they did so on separate planes. When they got there, Arthur Miller went straight to a hotel while Marilyn went to their apartment. Their marriage was over.

As was the norm, the press besieged the Millers' apartment building hoping to get a glimpse of Marilyn or better still a word from her. She was mostly invisible except for sessions with her psychiatrist, meanwhile every newspaper in America, as well as overseas, was discussing her marriage break-up. With her life becoming increasingly tense, Marilyn told 20th Century-Fox she would not appear in *Goodbye, Charlie* (Debbie Reynolds did instead) and then immediately after Christmas she went to Mexico for a vacation.

While Marilyn was away on vacation, her lawyer filed for her divorce from Arthur Miller. It was done on the same day as John F. Kennedy was inaugurated as President; it was a good day to bury bad news. Ten days later, Marilyn attended the World Premiere of *The Misfits* at the Granada Theater, Reno on 31 January, accompanied by one of her co-stars, Montgomery Clift. Arthur Miller was there too, but they avoided each other.

'Miller Walks Out On Marilyn.'
~ New York Daily News headline, 12 November 1960

The Misfits (1961)

Arthur Miller's very first screenplay is a modern-day cowboy story set in Nevada in which Gay Langland, a somewhat over-the-hill cowhand, is introduced to divorcee Roslyn by his friend Guido. Langland and Guido sell wild horses for dog food. Enter Perce Howland, a rodeo rider, and the three men and one woman combination proves to be a somewhat combustible scenario. In the end, Roslyn and Langland decide to make a go of it together, despite him being old enough to be her father.

'Marilyn plays a role into which are written bits and pieces reminiscent of her own life.' ~ *Life*

Clark Gable had a heart attack two days after filming ended; ten days later he died. There are claims that performing his own horse-riding and wrangling stunts was what killed him. It was Gable's last film, as it was to be Marilyn's. The irony of her relationship with Miller, how it played out in the desert, and the added poignancy of Gable being Marilyn's childhood screen hero, should not be forgotten. Inge Morath, who was hired to take the on-set photographs, ended up marrying Arthur Miller. It was a relationship that lasted 40 years.

'Characters and theme do not congeal. There is a lot of absorbing detail in it, but it doesn't add up to a point.' ~ *The New York Times*

CAST & CREDITS

Clark Gable – Gay Langland
Marilyn Monroe – Roslyn Taber
Montgomery Clift – Perce Howland
Thelma Ritter – Isabelle Steers
Eli Wallach – Guido

Director – John Huston
Producer – Frank Taylor
Screenplay – Arthur Miller
Music – Alex North
Cinematography – Russell Metty
Studio – United Artists

★ **THE MISFITS.** — Clark Gable, Marilyn Monroe, Montgomery Clift and a very competent cast enhance their acting reputations in this story. It's about a pampered divorcee who gets mixed up with a bunch of truck-riding cowboys earning a dubious living by catching wild misfit horses and selling them as dogs' meat. But it's not in the unforgettable class.—(A.) London Pavilion.

Marilyn Monroe and Montgomery Clift arrive at the Granada Theater, Reno, for the World Premiere of *The Misfits*, 31 January 1961

DECLINE

'Perhaps the quality that many people find attractive in her is her very insecurity, her unhappiness, her sleep-walking through life.' ~ **Ezra Goodman, from The Fifty Year Decline and Fall of Hollywood**

WHEN THE FIRST REVIEWS of *The Misfits* appeared they were overwhelmingly critical, and they singled out Marilyn in particular. It was not what she needed to hear and it was soon after this that she entered a psychiatric hospital in New York. She had finally broken. Memories of her childhood haunted her; she had, over the years, told virtually everyone close to her – friends, lovers, and co-stars – about how she had a crazy mother. Later reports speak of her behaving bizarrely in hospital while at the same time trying to convince friends who visited her that she was not mad. It was Joe DiMaggio who came to her rescue. He persuaded the medics to release Marilyn from the psychiatric hospital and transfer her to another New York hospital.

She was in hospital for three weeks, during which time friends say she grew increasingly listless. Her condition seemed to run soul-deep, and as every day passed so 20th Century-Fox grew increasingly anxious that their star should get back to work. As she got no better, it was DiMaggio who was once again on hand to help. This time he invited Marilyn to Florida, where he was living and working at the Yankees' training establishment. After a couple of weeks Marilyn, feeling much better physically, if not properly recovered mentally, returned to New York.

Waiting for Marilyn was a letter from 20th Century-Fox telling her to report to the studio right away. Toward the end of April Marilyn flew to Los Angeles, and accompanying her was Paula Strasberg who was once again back in the frame.

Meetings dragged on between Marilyn's agents and Fox, Marilyn being the pawn in their corporate game. Much of the debate hinged on who was to direct her next movie. Marilyn had originally given the studio a list of directors that she was prepared to work with, one of whom was Lee Strasberg. Fox were unhappy but Marilyn and MCA were contractually in the right. It all ended with Marilyn not being forced to make *Goodbye, Charlie*. Fox knew that if they went to court they could well lose.

While all this was playing itself out, Marilyn spent time in Palm Springs at Frank Sinatra's house. She also went to Las Vegas, where Sinatra was performing at the Sands, and partied with the Rat Pack and other Hollywood glitterati, including Elizabeth Taylor. Among those she met was Rat Pack original Peter Lawford, who also happened to be married to Pat Kennedy, brother of America's new President. Marilyn spent time at the Lawfords' home, but shortly after her 35th birthday she went back to New York for surgery on her gall bladder. She stayed back East for close to two months before returning to Hollywood in August.

COME FLY WITH ME... TO THE SANDS HOTEL!

Marilyn, Elizabeth Taylor, and Mr and Mrs Dean Martin watch Joey Bishop and Frank Sinatra at the Sands, Las Vegas, 8 June 1961

SUSPENSION

THE MOVE BACK TO California was not just a physical shift away from Arthur Miller's world, her marriage, and the life that she had thought she could carve out for herself when she first went to live with Milton Greene. In California she stayed in the homes of friends who were temporarily out of town, before moving into a small apartment. She knew she had to work as she was obligated to 20th Century-Fox to make a movie. Getting out of *Goodbye, Charlie* was just a temporary respite. She grew ever closer to her psychiatrist, Dr. Ralph Greenson, who, if anyone could, might just be able to dispel the demons and get her mind straightened out. Not that Marilyn was a lot of help to herself, because drink and drugs were still way too prevalent in her life. They helped to maintain the spiral of decline which she had entered long before she divorced Arthur Miller.

Marilyn, despite what seemed like a desire to escape her situation, was all too quick to put herself in trouble's path. Parties were the catalyst and she was regularly seen at the Lawfords' home. One evening in the early fall of 1961 she was invited to dinner at 625 Beach Road, their luxurious Santa Monica home, where the guest of honor was to be Attorney General Robert Kennedy, the President's brother. The night ended with Marilyn drunk and being driven home and put to bed, alone, by Kennedy and an aide.

Two weeks later, Marilyn was given another film role. It was a remake of a 1939 comedy that Fox was calling *Something's Got To Give*. Because she knew she could not refuse, it brought on yet more depression, not least because it was to be directed by George Cukor with whom she had made *Let's Make Love*. Things became so bad that her psychiatrist put her under round-the-clock care from a team of nurses. As the arguments with Fox dragged on, Marilyn went from living to existing. There were those close to her that doubted whether she was really fit enough to be able to complete a film.

Yet, what Marilyn needed to do more than anything was to work. Without her career she had no hope; she was not financially insecure, just emotionally ravaged. Some people need to work to make money, Marilyn needed to work to regain her self respect. Arguably she also needed to get the respect of others. As things panned out, Cukor was still finishing another picture for a rival studio and so things dragged on, which only served to increase Marilyn's propensity for insecurity. Finally it seemed that all was ready. Marilyn was due to report for filming in the middle of November and for once Fox were optimistic that she would. But Marilyn failed to show up and her co-star, Dean Martin, was left twiddling his thumbs. Fox yet again suspended her for breach of contract.

PRESIDENTIAL AID

'Subject reportedly spent some time with Robert Kennedy at the home of Peter Lawford in Hollywood. Subject reportedly challenged Mr. Kennedy on some points proposed to her by Miller.' ~ **Memorandum of 6 March 1962 in the FBI files**

IT SEEMS THAT during the previous twelve months an affair of sorts had begun with President Kennedy. Numerous sources have since spoken of it, although it was an infrequent sexual relationship rather than what many would regard as a full-blown affair. Given his position, the security surrounding him, and Marilyn's state of health it had to have been a sporadic relationship at best.

At the same time, or possibly later in 1961, it appears that Marilyn may also have been having sex with Robert Kennedy. It seems this relationship, like that with the President, should not really be called an affair. It was more like casual sex. However, a search of the available FBI files relating to Marilyn Monroe show that they are conspicuously thin for this period of her life. What little there is refers to Marilyn challenging Robert Kennedy over political issues. There is one memorandum from an unnamed source that makes lurid claims of sex parties where both Kennedys were in attendance, sometimes together, sometimes separately. The FBI case officer claims they cannot evaluate the authenticity of these statements. Evidence suggests there are unreleased FBI files that cover Marilyn; if they ever see the light of day much more will be revealed.

The FBI under J. Edgar Hoover was nothing if not thorough. Throughout most of this time Marilyn was still seeing her psychiatrist regularly, for periods it was every day. During this period she most definitely went to parties where JFK was in attendance, and not just on the West Coast but also in New York. There are also those who speculate that during this time she also had a relationship with Frank Sinatra. On top of all that there were ongoing arguments with 20th Century-Fox over the script, casting, cameraman, and just about every other aspect related to the making of *Something's Got to Give*. As 1961 became 1962, Marilyn was getting no nearer to making the film but it was inching closer almost imperceptibly.

Finally, something happened to help to break the deadlock. Fox suggested that Nunnally Johnson, who was living in Britain at the time, should do some work on the script. He was one writer she trusted as he had written the screenplay for *How To Marry A Millionaire*. Marilyn and her agent knew that time was beginning to work against her. The old adage that in Hollywood you're only as good as your last movie was for Marilyn very true. The failure of *The Misfits*, almost a year ago, was beginning to play on her mind. She needed a hit.

Robert Kennedy and his brother, President John F. Kennedy

BIRTHDAY GIRL

'I guess I'm reporting back.'
~ Marilyn at the Golden Globe Awards, 5 March 1962

IN FEBRUARY 1962 Arthur Miller remarried. His new wife, Inge Morath, was the stills photographer who worked on *The Misfits*. Friends of Marilyn have suggested that right up until their wedding she still harbored a fantastic notion that she and Miller could reunite. Marilyn was with Miller's father in Florida when she heard about the wedding. She then spent a few days with Joe DiMaggio before flying to Mexico City and then to Taxco for a vacation, which according to FBI files was arranged by Frank Sinatra. Home from Mexico in early March, Marilyn went to the Golden Globes at the Beverly Hilton Hotel at which she was given a 'World Film Favorite' award; her escort was Mexican writer Jose Bolanos. Marilyn wore a stunning green backless dress and a pair of diamond earrings given to her by Frank Sinatra.

BING CROSBY'S PALM DESERT HOME

Before March was over, Marilyn went to Palm Desert to a party at Bing Crosby's home. President Kennedy had been due to spend the night at Sinatra's home on Frank Sinatra Drive in Palm Springs – 'The Voice' had even begun to refer to it as the 'West Coast White House.' However, Robert Kennedy saw JFK and Sinatra's relationship as one fraught with potential pitfalls; others have said it was the Secret Service that vetoed Kennedy staying in Frank's home. Sinatra had modified his house to accommodate the Presidential entourage and it infuriated him when they decided not to stay with him. Instead, the President went to stay with Bing Crosby in Palm Desert, and Marilyn stayed there too.

Meanwhile, arguments continued over the script. Marilyn consulted Lee Strasberg and talked with her psychiatrist and friends. While she thought Nunnally's script was better, it was still not what she wanted. By late April Marilyn had caught a cold and so filming was postponed. Marilyn did finally start work at the very end of April but her attendance at the studio was erratic. The state of her mind was by then teetering on the brink. Dr Greenson left for a holiday in Europe with his wife. Her support system was shot.

There was barely enough filming going on in May to warrant the term; Marilyn had worked for just one full day. Then to cap it all, Marilyn announced that she was going to New York for a few days, for no other reason than to sing at Madison Square Garden. It was not a concert, but a gala celebration to honor President Kennedy's 45th birthday. Fox were naturally furious. It was all costing the ailing studio a fortune.

"Happy birthday, Mr President." Marilyn sings for John F. Kennedy, Madison Square Garden, New York City, 19 May 1962

FALL

'Fame stirs up envy.
Who does she think she is? Marilyn Monroe?'
~ Marilyn's last interview with Life magazine

MARILYN LEFT FOR New York late on in the day on Thursday 17 May, and upon arrival she headed for the apartment she still kept in the city. The next day, after getting up late she spent the afternoon rehearsing the song she was going to sing. Marilyn was to be the evening's finale, following, among others, opera diva Maria Callas and America's greatest living female singer, Ella Fitzgerald. Come Saturday night, her performance of 'Happy Birthday' for the President redefined sexy. It was not just her delivery, but the way she acted it out by running her hands all over her body. One columnist described her performance as "making love to the President in full view of America."

Some have called it a very public attempt at seduction. Others have called it a cry for help. In the world of amateur psychology it has been seen as an attempt to prove that she really was 'a good girl,' not the bad girl her former husbands had seen her as. It also put Marilyn back in the spotlight from which she had been drifting too far through her lack of film work. On the face of it, it was a great career move.

Back at work in Hollywood by the middle of the following week, Marilyn for once turned up on time for what was her most outrageous film scene ever – she was going to skinny-dip. She was a week or so shy of her 36th birthday and strangely, instead of trying to be seen as the actor she wanted to be, she had resorted to using her body. It only makes sense if you assume that Marilyn at this point was desperate. In one respect she was desperate; desperate to talk to the President. However, since her very public display of affection he had withdrawn back to Washington, not only because he did after

all have one of the biggest jobs in the world to do, but also because he could not afford a scandal like Marilyn.

There can be little doubt that President Kennedy was well aware of Marilyn's fragile personality and how someone like Marilyn could bring his house down, both personally with Jackie Kennedy, who had not attended the Madison Square Garden event in full knowledge that Marilyn would be there, and through the embarrassment he could bring to the office of President.

The President did not call to wish Marilyn a happy birthday and in the following days she went into an increasing decline. She was taking barbiturates and was comatose on some days. Fortunately, Ralph Greenson was due back any day from his European vacation – it couldn't be a day too soon. Behind the scenes in Hollywood, 20th Century-Fox were getting ready to fire Marilyn. Their relationship was not working and it was costing them a fortune every day she failed to show up for work. A week after Marilyn's birthday, Fox told her she was no longer required for *Something's Got to Give*; they followed it up by suing her for $750,000.

Marilyn's lawyers and her agent desperately tried to salvage the situation but Fox were adamant, and not content with firing Marilyn they suspended the film altogether. Days later, *Life* magazine had Marilyn all over its cover and hinted at the troubles with her movie. As if all this were not enough there was a power struggle going on at Fox as the studio's financial troubles deepened, with executives vying for control. Even Darryl F. Zanuck was being touted as the studio's new head.

Ironically, the doubts expressed by *Life* magazine over

Something's Got To Give, and most importantly the nude photograph of Marilyn, had excited public interest in her film. Fox were beginning to have second thoughts about firing her; perhaps they should just plough on with the film. Such were the studio's internal problems that most movies had been shut down but by mid-July Marilyn was back to work, although with a new director as Cukor had got a better offer. Ten days later Marilyn's old nemesis, Zanuck, had returned to 20th Century-Fox. Only time would tell how this would play out for Marilyn.

Ralph Greenson had been attending to Marilyn almost daily since his return from vacation and he was the rock, and just about the only one, that Marilyn could rely on. Her publicist, Pat Newcombe, was in daily attendance but she could do nothing to stem the intake of drugs. Marilyn always had plenty of barbiturates in her home but she had become more devious at getting extra supplies.

On Saturday 4 August Ralph Greenson went to see Marilyn during the day. Apart from being upset that her publicist had slept too long, she seemed fine. Pat Newcombe, who had stayed the previous night at Marilyn's apartment, left in the early evening, as did Greenson who had a dinner date. Marilyn was upset he couldn't stay, and around 7:30pm she telephoned him while he was shaving to tell him Joe DiMaggio's son had called her. Peter Lawford also called Marilyn, inviting her to dinner, but she declined. Lawford later said her speech was slurred. As the evening wore on there were other calls, including one from Jose Belanos, who said he thought she sounded fine. Marilyn called a girlfriend at around 10pm and invited her over but she said no, it was too late.

Marilyn, according to the funeral directors, died sometime between 9:30pm and 11:30pm. Her maid, unable to raise her but seeing a light under her locked door, called the police shortly after midnight. She also called Ralph Greenson who, on arrival, could not break down the bedroom door. He eventually broke in through French windows and found Marilyn dead in bed. The coroner stated she had died from acute barbiturate poisoning, and it was a 'probable suicide.'

MARILYN'S LEGACY

'She had suffered from psychiatric disturbances for a long time. She experienced severe fears and frequent depressions.'
~ A psychiatrist at the inquest into Marilyn's death

THE DAY AFTER MARILYN DIED was when it all began. It continued for weeks afterwards and is still going strong today. Speculation, gossip, titillation, and out-and-out voyeurism surrounded Marilyn's short life and her tragic death. Her death in particular has spawned conspiracy theories that include, among others, JFK, Sinatra, the Mafia, the CIA, and the FBI, and that is to just name the main players.

Many newspapers ran headlines the day after her death along the lines of 'Marilyn Monroe – It Looks Like Suicide.' That is what the coroner felt and the balance of all reasonable evidence since still points to that. She had been unwell for a long time, her mind had clearly been extremely unsettled, and when coupled with prodigious amounts of drugs that's a lethal combination. However, this book is not about trying to rake over the past in such a way

as to come to yet another conclusion. It's much more a celebration of her life.

First though, Marilyn needed a funeral and it was once again Joe DiMaggio who dealt with much of what needed to be done. It took place at the Westwood Funeral Chapel on Wednesday 8 August, and Marilyn had been placed in a green dress and platinum wig in an open casket. Joe DiMaggio, accompanied by his son, led the mourners. Mostly they were close friends, including Lee Strasberg and Marilyn's publicist, housekeeper, and attorney. DiMaggio excluded everyone from 'Hollywood.' In death, as in life, Marilyn was on the outside.

Arguably Marilyn was one of the first superstars to be attended by the full might of the media, including television. Bruce Johnston of the Beach Boys was close to Westwood cemetery on the day that Marilyn was buried. He recalled seeing helicopters circling overhead

'I am not interested in money. I just want to be wonderful.'
~ Marilyn

'Marilyn was history's most phenomenal love goddess.'
~ **Philippe Halsman, photographer**

trying to take photographs. It was probably the first time that the full-scale media circus came into play at the death of an icon, a superstar. For weeks afterwards there were more and more stories concerning Marilyn's death and the circumstances surrounding it. That was just the beginning.

It was Lee Strasberg and Marianne Kris, Marilyn's New York psychiatrist, who were left the majority of Marilyn's estate. It was not just her personal items, there was also a substantial amount of money. She had received around $80,000 for her role in *Some Like It Hot* just a matter of weeks before she died. Lee Strasberg's widow, Anna, at a sale in New York in 1999, eventually sold the personal items that Marilyn left to her late husband. It was, with some justification, dubbed the 'Sale of the Century.'

The sale created a raft of conflicting emotions and feelings among those that knew Marilyn and those who adored her image and reputation. There were some fans who just wanted to own a 'piece of Marilyn' while others found the whole thing distasteful. Perhaps the most commonly shared feeling is that her personal effects should have been preserved in a museum. That would, of course, have meant no sale. In the event, the chances of 'ordinary fans' owning anything that belonged to Marilyn was out of most people's financial reach. The prices realized were way in excess of the estimates and in some cases they were absolutely mind-blowing.

A pair of jeans worn by Marilyn in *River of No Return* were bought by designer Tommy Hilfiger for $42,550, and the dress worn by Marilyn when she entertained U.S. troops in Korea reached $112,500. Mariah Carey bought Marilyn's white baby grand piano for $662,500, when it had been estimated to sell for $15,000. One of Marilyn's rings sold for $772,500, while one of her Golden Globe awards fetched $184,000. Even 18 necklaces that had been expected to fetch $800 sold for $36,800. The most expensive item was the dress Marilyn wore to sing 'Happy Birthday' to President Kennedy – it sold for $1,267,500. The sale certainly lived up to its billing.

In 2005, 200 more items that had belonged to Marilyn were offered for sale by Julien's Auction house in Los Angeles. Yet again, the prices realized were way in excess of the original estimates, even for items of seemingly little value. One of the most intriguing objects was a painting by Marilyn of a symbolic red rose. It is inscribed, "President Kennedy, Happy Birthday and again I say Happy Birthday. Always, Marilyn Monroe, June 1, 1962." It sold for $78,000 against an estimate of $10,000, which when compared to what had sold at the previous sale seems to be a relative bargain given its double connection. A tan three-ring bound telephone book with the numbers of Marilyn's friends, including Montgomery Clift, Joe DiMaggio, Henry Fonda, Peter Lawford, Jack Lemmon, Arthur Miller, Yves Montand, and Frank Sinatra, sold for a staggering $90,000.

Ironically, everything she had touched was worth more in death than in life.

'I want to grow old without facelifts. I want to have the courage to be loyal to the face I have made.'
~ Marilyn

'I don't mind living in a man's world as long as I can be a woman in it.' ~ **Marilyn**

In a way that's exactly what Marilyn has done. She died before she got old and so our memory is of her beauty and her image, a vision that is unsullied by the passage of time. It's not just from the movies and from photographs of Marilyn that we remember her. For every Elvis Presley lookalike and impersonator in the world there are probably two or three 'Marilyns.' Countless events, parties, trade shows, and marketing campaigns have a Marilyn impersonator. Sadly, and of course inevitably, most of them look little like the real thing. Marilyn was a lot more than blonde and red lipstick, yet for most people all they know is that image, the illusion fabricated by Hollywood.

'Marilyn is a kind of ultimate. She is uniquely feminine.'
~ **Clark Gable**

'It's a terrible pity that so much beauty has been lost to us.'
~ **John Huston**

'When you look at Marilyn on the screen, you don't want anything bad to happen to her.'
~ **Natalie Wood**

'As an actress, she has lots of imitators – but only Marilyn survives.' ~ **Eli Wallach**

'I would rather work with her than any other actress. I adore her.' ~ **Montgomery Clift**

The last word will be Marilyn's…

'I knew I belonged to the public and to the world, not because I was talented or even beautiful, but because I had never belonged to anything or anyone else.'

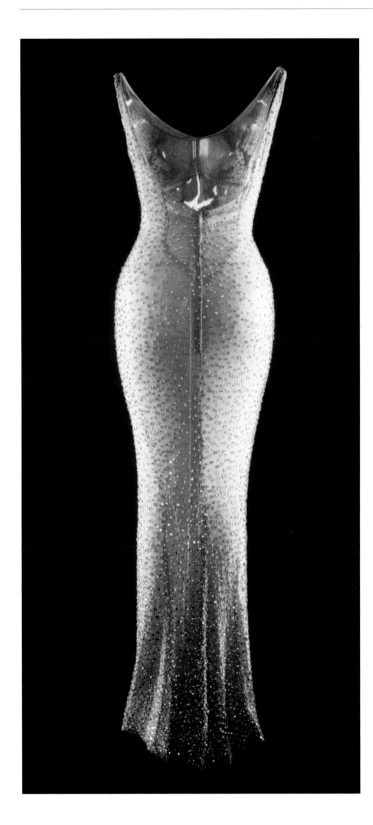

In 2016 proof—if it were necessary—of Marilyn's continued veneration as Hollywood royalty came over three days and a thousand lots at Julien's auction house in Beverly Hills. Many of the intimate possessions came from the estate of her friend and acting coach, Lee Strasberg, to whom she bequeathed her clothes and many personal effects; others from collector David Gainsborough-Roberts, who had amassed a fabled collection of the costumes Marilyn wore in her film roles.

And, indeed, many of the items auctioned were related to her movies: the cocktail dress she wore in *Some Like it Hot*; the green satin one-piece with black sequins and gold fringe worn in *Bus Stop*; rhinestone earrings from *How To Marry A Millionaire*, along with many others. Marilyn had few expensive bits of jewelry, preferring to achieve a dramatic effect with costume pieces, but one of the few expensive items was sold: a ladies platinum and diamond cocktail watch. Other lots included a 1947 Revlon lipstick, handbags, letters and sketches, checkbooks and tax documents.

The pièce de resistance, however, was the Jean Louis dress that Marilyn wore when she sang "Happy birthday, Mr President" to President John F. Kennedy at New York's Madison Square Garden. Designed by Bob Mackie, then 21 years old and fresh out of college, it cost $12,000 in 1962, made $1.26 million at auction in 1999, and in 2016 was sold for $4.8 million—beating into second place Marilyn's white costume from *The Seven Year Itch* which went for $4.6 million in 2011. Auction house CEO Darren Julien named the Jean Louis dress "the most historic, important piece of Marilyn Monroe that could ever be offered." Edward Meyer, vice president of the purchaser, Ripley's Believe It Or Not Museum, told the Press Association:

"We believe this is the most iconic piece of pop culture that there is. In the 20th century I cannot think of one single item that tells the story of the 1960s as well as this."

Marilyn sings to JFK, May 19, 1962.

FURTHER READING

'She will go on eternally.' ~ **Jackie Kennedy Onassis**

IN THE DIGITAL AGE there is no greater testament to celebrity than the number of web sites or the number of Google hits that someone achieves – when you type in 'Marilyn Monroe' you get 'about 12,600,000' hits. Not bad for someone who passed away almost 50 years ago. Incidentally, Elvis Presley does a little better at 16.1 million hits, The Beatles get close to 50 million; Marilyn's idol Jean Harlow can barely muster half a million.

Naturally, the number of sites worth visiting that have interesting content about Marilyn is way fewer than 12.6 million. Among the best are:

www.marilyncollector.com
As the banner says, 'Keeping the legend alive.'

One of the best sites is www.marilynmonroe.ca
which has had over a million visitors since 2000.

There's also www.marilynmonroe.com which is less interesting than one would expect for 'the official site.'

An interesting blog can be found at
themarilynmonroecollection.blogspot.com

www.immortalmarilyn.com does exactly what it says –
it helps to immortalize Marilyn and is well worth visiting.

www.marilynmonroepages.com is another great tribute,
as is www.marilynremembered.org

Lastly, there's the FBI files on Marilyn at
http://foia.fbi.gov/foiaindex/monroe.htm

All these web sites were looked at and consulted during the creation of this book. And of course don't forget YouTube, although be careful, you could get lost in there!

There have been countless books already on Marilyn. Many of them were consulted during the writing of this book; among them were:

My Story by Marilyn Monroe with Ben Hecht.

The Many Lives of Marilyn Monroe by Sarah Churchwell.

Inside Marilyn Monroe – A Memoir by John Gillmore.

Norma Jean: The Life of Marilyn Monroe by Fred Lawrence Guiles.

Marilyn Monroe: A Biography by Barbara Leeming.

My Sister Marilyn by Mona Rae Miracle.

Marilyn Monroe: An Intimate Personal Account by Lena Pepitone.

Goddess: The Secret Lives of Marilyn Monroe by Anthony Summers.

The Secret Life of Marilyn Monroe by J. Randy Taraborrelli.

INDEX

THE WITHOUT WHOM DEPARTMENT
As usual, without Christine Havers, Bruce Johnston and Shelley Faye Lazar this book would not have been possible. Thanks also to Melinda Mason at www.marilynmonroe.ca, Derek Anthony in Los Angeles, and the fabulous Doctor Macro (www.doctormacro.info).